The Size of the World and Other Plays

By Charles Evered

ISBN: 1-57502-670-8

Library of Congress Catalog Card Number: 97-77650

Artwork by: Gerald Bergstrom

Published by Billings/Morris, Ltd. UK. Printed in the United States by: Morris Publishing • 3212 East Highway 30 • Kearney, NE 68847

MORRIS PUBLISHING

Louis Zorich, Rita Moreno and Frank Whaley
in *The Size of the World*, by Charles Evered.

Photo: Gerry Goodstein

More praise for Charles Evered's "The Size of the World and Other Plays"...

"It does not happen often enough that we find a writer willing to probe with new sensibilities the theme of family, which has been the fixation of many of this century's great plays. Charles Evered has done so, and his work evokes an entirely new approach to grappling with the illusions that so many of us use to get by. He does so with moving humanity, with wry comedy, and with a provocative conclusion, and his style and manner may also tell us something significant about where we are."

Milan Stitt, Playwright, *The Runner Stumbles* and Chairman, Yale University Writing Program

"Last night I dreamed about some of Chuck's characters. And when you dream about Chuck's characters, you have to dream about their "manic panic," and their jittery despair. But, the funny thing is that I dreamed about them and awoke refreshed! That is the effect they have on you, which is another way of saying that Chuck Evered... is an artist."

Austin Pendleton, Actor/Playwright, *Booth, Uncle Bob*

"No other artist, other than perhaps Bruce Springsteen, has quite captured as Chuck Evered has, the gnawed, frayed and dismayed emotional pulse of a lost, but very prevalent creature of the American landscape -- those who hover like neglected shadows in our strip malls, parking lots, and the fading artery towns off the New Jersey Turnpike."

Bonnie J. Monte, Artistic Director, New Jersey Shakespeare Festival

A few words and many thanks...

Re-visiting these plays has been an amazing experience. All written when I was between the ages of 18 and 24, they recall a time when everything seemed in flux, and when I was searching for a means to express what we all tend to experience during those formative years; a thirst to find out who we are, what sort of voice we have, (if any), and most importantly, finding out what matters to us.

I think what struck me most by reacquainting myself with the people in these stories, was that the "person" who wrote them so clearly identified with those who live in what might be termed the "periphery." In fact, if this collection of plays had a sub-title, it very well might have been "Outside Big Cities," because they almost all take place in the shadow of a bigger place, and are peopled with characters who live their lives quietly underneath those shadows.

I've also been able to take some time to look back and marvel at how fortunate I've been to have achieved even the small success I have. Writing these plays helped order my thoughts and emotions during times in which I needed to make some sense of things. The fact that so many accomplished people were willing to champion, promote, and in some instances, even sponsor my work, has been icing on a cake that initially, wasn't even baked for anyone else's consumption.

To that end, I have many people to thank. Firstly, my parents Charles and Marie Evered for being extraordinary people. Also, my sisters Anne Evered and Kathleen Mangano for their belief in me. In addition, my brother Daniel Cole Evered, Marion Ophees, Mark Mangano and my aunt and uncle; Eileen and Larry Flanagan. Also, to my nephews and nieces, who make me very proud; Gabe Evered, Megan Grippa, Julie Grippa, Anthony Grippa Jr. and Marie Mangano.

To Miss Kerry Kennedy for being a reminder of what a real writer is. Also, thanks to Frank Favata, Rob Nissen, Rob Jacklosky and everyone at The Othersyde Theatre Company.

Thanks as well to my spiritual fathers; Ron Bosland, Milan Stitt, George Roy Hill and Austin Pendleton.

Many thanks to many fine directors. Among them; Elizabeth Margid, Walt Jones, Steve Campo, Anne Justine D'Zmura, John Basinger, Mark Rucker, Joe Brancato, Anastasia Traina and Bonnie J. Monte.

To a long list of actors, all of whom have honored me with their talent. Especially; Peter Gregory, Scott Cohen and William Francis McGuire for their belief in and support of "Billy and Dago." Also, Damian Young, Sean Cullen, Olympia Dukakis, Louis Zorich, Mary Fogarty, Nick Brooks, Luke Perry, Paul Giamatti, Liev Schreiber, Frank Whaley, Gus Rogerson, Joshua Fardon and Rita Moreno.

Many thanks also to Arthur Miller, Hassan Ildari, Little Storm, Davina Belling, Sarah Fargo, Bill Wrubel, Paul Zimmerman and Hugh Thomas.

Lots of thanks as well to the producers who put their money where their mouths were; Charles and Ann Rucker, Don and Grace Pitti, Lloyd Richards and Ethan Hawke.

And finally, to my representatives; Alan Gasmer, Mike Lubin, Betsy Helf and Mary Meagher, for still believing in stories about people.

Charles Evered
November 14, 1997
Ho Chi Minh City, (Saigon)

THE PLAYS

THE SIZE OF THE WORLD
TRACES
BILLY AND DAGO
IT'S KINDA LIKE MATH
ONE CALL
RUNNING FUNNY
PAPER KLIPS

THE SIZE OF THE WORLD

To Stan and Rita Kamin

THE SIZE OF THE WORLD was first produced in a workshop at The Yale School of Drama with the following cast:

Peter Hogancamp: Sean Cullen
Vivian Merkel: Zoey Zimmerman
Stan Merkel: Joseph Fuqua

The director was Elizabeth Margid.

The play was given its first professional production as part of "Winterfest" at Yale Repertory Theatre with:

Peter Hogancamp: Liev Schreiber
Vivian Merkel: Mary Fogarty
Stan Merkel: Conrad McLaren

The director was Walton Jones.

The play was subsequently produced at Circle Repertory Theater, New York City with:

Peter Hogancamp: Frank Whaley
Vivian Merkel: Rita Moreno
Stan Merkel: Louis Zorich

The director was Austin Pendleton.

The Characters

PETER HOGANCAMP: Twenties

VIVIAN MERKEL: Sixties

STAN MERKEL: Sixties

The Setting and Time

The play takes place in the kitchen of an aluminum sided house in Passaic, New Jersey.

The time is the present.

Act One, Scene One

(As the lights come up, we see Peter in the center of the kitchen with a beat up suitcase in his hand. Stan and Vivian face him)

PETER: I'm a public speaker.
STAN: What is that?
PETER: You know --
VIVIAN: -- you make speeches?
PETER: Yeah. In public. I teach people how to talk in public.
VIVIAN: What do you talk about?
PETER: Talking. How to do it. I talk about how to do something at the same time as I'm doing it.
STAN: How do you make money doin' that?
PETER: I charge people. I have classes.
VIVIAN: So, you're a teacher?
PETER: Yeah, sort of. Yeah.
VIVIAN: The rent's three twenty a month, honey.
PETER: Three twenty is good.
STAN: Hey, wait a minute here --
VIVIAN: -- do you wanna look at the room now?
STAN: --hey--
PETER: -- it doesn't matter. Does it have a bed?
STAN: --hey, hold your --
VIVIAN: -- sure it has a bed.
PETER: That's good.
STAN: Alright, hold your --
VIVIAN: -- and it's very clean.
PETER: I'm sure it is. (Looks) The kitchen's very clean.
STAN: Hey, just hold on a minute here!
VIVIAN: Stanley, just let 'im talk. He seems like a nice boy to me.
STAN: I'm tryin' to give him a chance here! (Pause) Are ya workin' now or what?

PETER: Yeah sure, I'm always workin'. I'm always workin'.

VIVIAN: Tell Stanley where ya work, honey.

PETER: Well, I don't go to a job. It's more like wherever I go the job is, since I'm the only one doin' it.

STAN: What does that mean?

PETER: It means... you know. I have classes and symposiums and stuff...that I set up...wherever I happen to be.

STAN: Where was your last ... "symposium?"

PETER: It was here, at the Y. That's where I was stayin' up till now...just for a little while...I was kind of in what they call a "transitional" stage in my life.

STAN: What is that?

PETER: It's...I wasn't gonna stay there for long. It's not a bad place. People think of people stayin' at the Y like they're a bunch of losers, but they're not. The Y's still a good place. It's respectable. You know, clean sheets and stuff.

VIVIAN: Is this where ya grew up?

PETER: Yeah, mostly.

STAN: Where?

PETER: State Street. We had a house on the end of it.

VIVIAN: Oh, State! Isn't that nice, Stanley, State Street!

STAN: So why aren't you there now?

PETER: I can't be.

STAN: Why not?

PETER: Everybody's dead.

VIVIAN: Oh, I'm sor --

PETER: -- yeah, I'm not new to here or anything, but I moved around a lot. I only ended up at the Y because I didn't want to put anybody out. I have a lot of friends.

VIVIAN: Well, that's good. (Pause) How did ya get that scar over your eye, honey?

PETER: Oh. I was uh...I was bowling and uh, well, you know...I was bowling.

VIVIAN: Oh.

PETER: Yeah. Actually, all I need really is a kind of home base. I need a phone.

VIVIAN: We have a phone.
PETER: Great. And listen, I'm only gonna stay for as long as until I hook-up with an organization that I think will appreciate what I have to offer them. You know, my heightened sense of commitment and all that stuff...about what I do.
VIVIAN: Oh. Oh, boy. Isn't that somethin', Stanley?
STAN: What do you do again?
PETER: I'm a public speaker.
STAN: What kind of organization needs that?
PETER: Well, what I'm gonna do is set up a few meetings with the top people who head up the hotels in the city. You know, Hilton, Sheraton, all those type of places. Not the regular ones like out in the Meadowlands. I mean the big ones on The Rock, that's the city. That's where the corporate headquarters are usually. And what I figured I could do is tell them that I'm offering myself as a kind of entrepreneur. You know, in the sense that I could conduct some kind of seminars on public speaking. Like how to speak in public and in business meetings and lunches and stuff like that. See all the biggest hotels in the world have the biggest seminar rooms down-stairs. And I figured, why couldn't I become a regular or somethin'. Kind of the one person they have to go around talkin' to people about talking. And I could travel too, because they have hotels all over the place. I mean if they book singers and comics and all that, why can't they book somebody legitimate like me?
VIVIAN: Wow! You really can talk.
PETER: Yeah, ever since I was like one and a half. My father was an instructor in it.
VIVIAN: He was a public talker, too?
PETER: Yeah, but just around here.
STAN: How are you gonna get paid?
PETER: The hotels will pay me for doin' all this. That's how I'll make my money.
STAN: It don't sound too steady to me.

PETER: Well, it is. Why not? That's how I got here. How do you think I have money now?

STAN: How *do* ya have money now?

PETER: At the Y. I started just for the fun of it, you know, lookin' at all the old books my father gave me. (Peter refers to a couple of paperbacks in his pocket) "How to Win Friends and Influence People" and "Effective Speaking" and stuff like that. And just for the hell of it I started talkin' about it to the other people there... you know, in the T.V. room.

VIVIAN: Oh.

PETER: And before I knew it, everybody was lookin' at me. Not at the television. And they were sittin' in chairs in front of me, and I was standin' behind some old shelf, but it was like I was behind one of those lectern things. And I was talkin'. And they were listenin. And before I knew it, Jack, the guy who washes the towels got Mr. Kellerman to come down and see me. And he said I could do it as part of their "Self Affirmation Program."

VIVIAN: Well, that's somethin'.

PETER: And this is all just Passaic. Just imagine what could happen with some bigger place in the world that people actually heard about. "From little things," you know...

VIVIAN: Stanley's a historian.

STAN: Aaaah...

PETER: Oh, yeah? Wow.

STAN: Naa.

VIVIAN: Sure you are.

STAN: I'm an amateur historian.

PETER: Well, isn't that nice?

STAN: Your plan there...it sounds a little like it's in the air.

PETER: It's not.

VIVIAN: Tell 'im you were in the paper, Stanley.

STAN: Yeah, I was in the paper.

PETER: That's great. For what?

STAN: I made a discovery about the redcoats.

PETER: Well gee whiz, what was that?

VIVIAN: Tell 'im, Stanley.

STAN: They came across...they came across the old Main Street bridge....they were chasin' George Washington and I...some of our guys...the Americans...they burned down the bridge so they couldn't cross the river. And I discovered that. I researched it.

PETER: Wow. How very interesting. I'd like to hear a lot more about the revolutionaries back then in Passaic. It seems to me, and I'm not sure about this, Stan, you're the historian, but it seems to me that too many of us young Americans don't readily appreciate, exactly what all our forefathers did to preserve our freedom in this great land of ours. You know, without the blemish of tyranny, and all that stuff. (Pause)

STAN: Yeah. (Pause) Yeah.

VIVIAN: Oh, Stanley has a million stories about the old times. Stanley's lived here all his life.

STAN: Yeah. I lived here all my life.

VIVIAN: He was a roofer.

STAN: Yeah. I was a roofer.

PETER: How many of us go to bed at night, secure in the knowledge that we won't wake up sopping wet, because we're under a roof...that someone like you, Stan, built for us? (Pause)

STAN: I don't know.

(Peter takes Stan's hand, shakes it)

PETER: Thanks, Stan.

STAN: For what?

PETER: For doin' that. For putting up roofs day after day that thousands of people sleep under, and don't even appreciate.

STAN: Oh. Yeah, yeah. Well, that's okay.

VIVIAN: So, how long would you stay...what's your name again, dear?

PETER: Peter. Peter Hogancamp.

VIVIAN: Peter.

PETER: Well, for as long until I go. If that's okay with you.

STAN: Now wait a minute. Just hold on a minute here. We gotta talk about it.

PETER: Of course. When do ya think you'll know?

STAN: Just leave us your number.

VIVIAN: Maybe we could talk about it now.

PETER: Great. I'll just go in the other room. Do ya mind?

VIVIAN: Go ahead. (Peter exits into the house) Well, Stanley, it would be three twenty a month -- and we could use it.

STAN: I thought we were "thinkin'" about rentin' that room? This isn't thinkin' about it -- this is doin' it.

VIVIAN: Oh, I know. I know, I'm sorry, but he seems like such a nice boy, Stanley. And wouldn't it be nice to have a boy around the house again?

STAN: We gotta think about it first.

VIVIAN: Oh, I know -- but he can help out in the yard...and he could even take Kelly for walks if he wants to.

STAN: He sounds like a talker to me.

VIVIAN: But wouldn't it be nice to have somebody else talkin' around here but us?

STAN: I was just gettin' used to the quiet.

VIVIAN: Well, I can't get used to it, Stanley.

(Pause. Stanley considers for a moment, then...)

STAN: Tell 'im he has to pay up front.

VIVIAN: Okay.

(Vivian heads to the door)

STAN: Wait.

VIVIAN: What?

STAN: Tell 'im not to mess up the room. Tell 'im not to change anything around in the room.

VIVIAN: I will. (Pause) And thank you, Stanley. (She kisses Stan, then calls out...) Peter?

PETER: (Entering) Yes, Vivian?

VIVIAN: Ya have to pay up front!

PETER: Well, sure, sure. Where will I be stayin'?

VIVIAN: Oh, you'll be stayin' in Scott's old room.

STAN: My boy Scott is out in California.

VIVIAN: Yeah, he works in computers. He used to help us around the house, but...now he's out in California. There's a picture of him in the living room.

PETER: Oh yeah.

STAN: Yeah.

VIVIAN: Him and Stanley used to go rock huntin' up on Garret Mountain.

PETER: Wow. How very interesting. What kinda rocks da ya hunt, Stan?

STAN: Quartz mostly. All kinds.

PETER: How very nice.

VIVIAN: Him and Scott used to go every weekend.

PETER: Oh. (To Stan) Well, can you still see enough to --

VIVIAN: (Abrupt) -- Sh.

PETER: What?

VIVIAN: -- Sh!

STAN: What's going on?

VIVIAN: Nothing, Stanley. Go on upstairs and get Peter some sheets.

(Stan gets up, using an old baseball bat for a cane and heads into the house. Vivian quietly closes the door behind him)

PETER: Did I say something wrong, or --

VIVIAN: -- Stanley is blind, Peter.

PETER: I know. That's why I was --

VIVIAN: -- but I think it's better not to let him know.

PETER: (Pause) But he does know, right?

VIVIAN: Yes, but he doesn't have to know we know.

PETER: But he does know we know. We see him.

VIVIAN: I just don't think it's a very good thing to talk about, that's all.

PETER: (Pause) Oh...kay.

VIVIAN: Now, when ya take Kelly for a walk --

PETER: -- who's Kelly?

VIVIAN: Kelly is our dog.

PETER: Well, where is he?

VIVIAN: He's outside...in the back.

PETER: Oh, I didn't see 'im. What kind is he?

VIVIAN: He's dead.

PETER: I'm sorry?
VIVIAN: He's dead.
PETER: (After a pause) Then why do you still walk 'im?
VIVIAN: I only tell Stanley I do.
PETER: Ya mean he thinks his dog is...
VIVIAN: That's right.
(Vivian moves over to a houseplant on the window sill and presses her finger down on a tape recorder hidden behind it. We hear a dog bark a few times)
PETER: Oh, my God! That's sick!
VIVIAN: That's Kelly.
PETER: That's the *real* Kelly?
VIVIAN: My girlfriend Rose made a recording on the day we had to put 'im to sleep.
PETER: Oh, my God.
VIVIAN: Honey, don't make a big to-do about it. Just don't say anything.
PETER: Well, how long have ya --
VIVIAN: -- a couple of years. Stanley bought Kelly for Scott a long time ago.
PETER: Yeah, but Vivian, don't ya think it's kinda weird?
VIVIAN: Don't make a big to-do about it, Peter. It would break Stanley's heart. He's a good man.
PETER: Oh, I know, I'm sure, Vivian. I just think...see I'm not gonna be around much anyway. I'll mostly be in the city.
(Stan enters with the sheets)
STAN: Here ya go.
VIVIAN: Thank you, Stanley. Now take your medicine.
(Stan goes to the table to put drops in his eyes. Vivian takes the sheets)
STAN: So. When are you gonna start makin' your speeches?
PETER: Oh. I gotta go in tomorrow and do some research. You know, stake the places out and stuff.
STAN: "Public speakin'."
PETER: Yup.
VIVIAN: Do you wanna see your room now, honey?

PETER: Sure.
VIVIAN: Oh, and Stanley, Peter even fed Kelly for us...didn't
   you, dear?
PETER: What?
VIVIAN: Kelly?
PETER: Oh, yeah. Yeah. Nice doggy. Nice doggy.
   (Peter pets the air)
VIVIAN: C'mon, honey, I'll take ya up. Do ya like to take a
   shower in the mornin'?
PETER: Yeah.
VIVIAN: Let's go.

(Vivian exits into the house. Peter hesitates and stands in the
doorway, looking at Stan. Sensing Peter is there, Stan turns
toward him. Peter hurries away, up the stairs. Lights fade as
Stan looks toward the window)

Act One, Scene Two

   (As the lights come up, we see Stan seated while
   Vivian sets the table around him. Peter bursts through the
   door. Sees Stan and Vivian, and feeling as though
   he's intruded, backs up. Vivian stops him)

VIVIAN: Peter!
PETER: Vivian, sorry about --
VIVIAN: -- did you get the job?
PETER: Vivian, I told ya. There isn't so much a job for me to
   get, as there is a job I have to give somebody the chance to give
   me.
VIVIAN: Oh, yeah. Yeah.
STAN: Where were ya?
PETER: It was just a scouting run. Checking out places...size,
   scope...stuff like that.
VIVIAN: Well, did ya talk to anybody?

PETER: Oh, yeah. I did good today. I mean I made a lota
contacts. But, like I said, it was more or less just research. I
have to see if these places have the facilities first.
VIVIAN: Well, sit down, honey. Have some supper.
PETER: Oh, no thanks, Vivian.
(Vivian puts the third plate filled with food on the table)
VIVIAN: It's all right, honey. I bought a bigger chicken -- just for
you.
PETER: You mean you want me to eat *with* you. Sitting down
and everything?
VIVIAN: Sure.
PETER: Am I gonna have to pay extra?
VIVIAN: No, honey, supper is in the rent.
STAN: Just supper.
PETER: Oh. Okay. Thanks. (Peter sits down at the table, wary)
It's just been awhile since I ate with people. I mean sitting next
to them and everything.
(Peter stands)
STAN: What's the matter with you?
PETER: Nothin' I just...Vivian, what kind of impression am I
making on you right now?
STAN: Sit down.
VIVIAN: What do ya mean?
PETER: I mean as impressions go, how would you say that I
impress you right now...good or bad?
STAN: Hey --
VIVIAN: -- good, I guess.
STAN: What's the matter with you?
PETER: Nothin'. Forget it, forget it.
(Peter sits reluctantly. As soon as everyone starts to eat, he
stands again)
PETER: See, if I only coulda gotten that moron's name.
STAN: What's goin' on here?
VIVIAN: Whose name Peter?

PETER: The guy at the Sheraton. I walked into The Sheraton, you
know, no big deal or anything, just to inquire about the guy in
charge. I didn't say "guy in charge," I said manager or
somethin'. So this guy on the floor asks me what I wanted, like
I was a salesman or somethin', and I just tell 'im..."I'm here to
inquire about a possible future arrangement regarding the
organizational feasibility of running a public speaking seminar."
And he looks at me like he doesn't know what I'm talkin'
about. So then I thought to do what you should always do in
situations like that... talk about the person you are talkin' to, not
about yourself.

VIVIAN: You hear that, Stanley?

PETER: I mean I saw he was a little "iffy" about how he felt
about me, so I just did what you should always do when you
wanna get people to like ya. "Let people talk about themselves."
Like Stan, let me show ya. Say you're somebody I wanna get to
like me.

STAN: I'm eatin' here.

VIVIAN: Go ahead, Stanley.

PETER: Just try to imagine Stan, however hard it may be, that
you don't like me, okay...and I want ya to. So, I'd say
somethin' like; "Stan, that's a very nice name. What's that short
for?" And then you'd say....

STAN: I wouldn't say anything.

VIVIAN: Come on, Stanley, go along.

PETER: "Stan, well, that's a very nice name. What's that short
for?" And then you'd say...

STAN: (Reluctant) Stanley.

PETER: Right. And then I'd say, "Stanley, well, that's a very
nice name. Was your father named Stanley, also?" And then
you'd say...

STAN: Ah, come on.

VIVIAN: Go on, Stanley.

PETER: And then you'd say --

STAN: No, NO for cripe's sake!

PETER: There, see? See how I got you to talk about yourself without my havin' to talk about myself too much? That's what I tried to do with this guy. He looks at me like I'm a nobody, and so I ask 'im what his name is...you know, start gettin' 'im on the track of talkin' about himself, and he goes to me; "None of your business."

VIVIAN: Well, that wasn't very nice.

PETER: How are you supposed to act like you wanna get to know somebody when they act like they don't give a shit whether you act like you wanna get to know them or not? I didn't give a flying crap what this guy's name was. And he tells me it's none of my business. Well, fuck him!

STAN: Hey!

PETER: Sorry, Vivian.

STAN: (After a pause) What *was* his name?

PETER: I don't know. He didn't tell me. That's the point, Stan. If he told me what his name was, I coulda told 'im I thought it was nice.

VIVIAN: Well, who was he, honey?

PETER: Just some floor guy, that's all. But it's all right, live and learn. That's why to me, it was just a trial run. "If you persuade yourself that you can do a certain thing, provided this thing is possible, then you will do it."

VIVIAN: Wow. Who said that?

PETER: (As though a name) Anonymous.

STAN: Why can't we just eat here?

PETER: All right. All right.

(Peter sits again. Fiddles with his food, stands)

STAN: What is he doin'?

PETER: But ya know that talkin' about the other person stuff, that is only one facet of all the knowledge I encompass about what I'm talkin' about.

STAN: Hey, why can't you just sit down and eat?

VIVIAN: Stanley, let him talk.

PETER: It's what I do, Stan. I thought you wanted to know what I did.

VIVIAN: Go on, Peter.

PETER: Thank you, Vivian.

VIVIAN: You're welcome.

STAN: (Throws down fork) Oh, for Christ --

PETER: -- see, there are certain things an effective speaker must and must not do. And one of the things he must, is that after he has "strode forth bravely" to his podium, he must "perooze" his audience. Ya perooze 'em, and ya look at 'em like you're lookin' at a room fulla people that owe ya money.

STAN: Why do they owe ya money?

PETER: They don't, Stan, ya just look at 'em like they do.

VIVIAN: Oh.

PETER: Another thing is, when you're talkin' in front of alota people, it's a good idea, before ya say anything, to just...laugh a little...lightly.

STAN: Laugh?

PETER: Yeah. Lightly. Just a little "sprinkling of laughter." Not a big "Ha ha," just a little..."Huh huh."

STAN: What do ya wanna laugh in front of people for?

PETER: It puts 'em at ease.

STAN: What do ya wanna do that for?

PETER: Because ya wanna make 'em like ya.

STAN: Why do ya wanna make 'em like ya, if they owe ya money?

PETER: They don't owe me money, Stan.

STAN: You just said they did.

PETER: I said you gotta look at 'em like they did.

VIVIAN: Stanley.

STAN: Well, who's gonna like ya if you're laughin' at 'em?

PETER: I'm not...I'm not laughin' *at* them, Stan, like "Ha Ha." I'm laughin' lightly...in their presence...to give 'em the idea that I like 'em. You have to understand the nature of an audience, Stan. You have to stand there and look at 'em...not like they're a big group of people all together in one room...but a buncha separate individuals.

STAN: What's the difference?

PETER: Well, who do ya think it's easier to talk to ... a person, or a group of persons? (Pointing suddenly) Vivian!

VIVIAN: A person?

PETER: That's right. So to make it less like you're talkin' to a big group of people, ya talk to everybody like they're one person. Because what is a group of people, but a buncha "one persons" all together at the same time...in the same place?

STAN: What the hell is he talkin' about?

VIVIAN: Stanley --

PETER: -- now, when ya actually do say things, one of the most important things to remember, is to remember what ya should say...and what ya shouldn't say. And they have a saying to describe the kinds of words ya shouldn't say. And what is the word that describes what it is I shouldn't say? (Pointing quick) Stan!

STAN: I don't know --

PETER: -- weasel words!

STAN: What?

PETER: What you just said. They were "weasel words."

STAN: What did I say?

PETER: You didn't know.

STAN: I *didn't* know!

PETER: Weasel words. "I don't know...I don't think...I'm not sure...," they're all "weasel words."

STAN: Well, what am I supposed to say?

PETER: Anything. Just don't sound like you don't know what you're talkin' about.

STAN: But if I don't know what I'm talkin' about, how am I supposed to sound like I do?

PETER: There's an answer for that.

(Long pause as Peter fiddles his thumbs)

STAN: Well, what is it?

PETER: I just said it.

STAN: What?

PETER: You just asked me a question I didn't have an answer for, and instead of sayin' "I don't know," or "I'm not sure," I told ya there was an answer for it.
(Another long pause)
STAN: So what is it?
PETER: I didn't tell ya yet. I just said there was one...even though I didn't happen to know what it was myself. But the important thing was, in all of this, I've been answering questions I didn't have answers for, and I haven't had to say one single weasel word to do it.
STAN: What...what...WHAT -- !
PETER: (Gets up, prowling) -- see, the thing you have to remember when you're sayin' somethin' you're not sure of, is to move on to the next thing you're sayin' as quick as possible...before the people you're talkin' to realize that you didn't have any idea what the thing you were just talkin' about meant. Do ya know what I'm sayin? See this way, by the time you move on to the next thing, they've forgotten about whatever it was you were just talkin' about...even though you had no idea what it was yourself. Now do ya know what I'm talkin' about? (Pointing) Vivian!
VIVIAN: Well. (Pause) I'm not sure I --
PETER : -- weasel words! See, it's better to say nothin' than to let people know you don't know what you're talkin' about. A person can be two things when they're not talkin; a genius...or a fuckin' moron.
STAN: Hey!
PETER: And as soon as that person opens their mouth, they're automatically found out. Believe me, it's better to be thought of as a quiet genius, than to be known as a somewhat gregarious asshole with mediocre thoughts.
STAN: Are you tellin' me people pay you to teach this stuff?
PETER: Yeah. All this is a commodity. Like watches or whatever. I mean if a guy could sell watches, he could sell this kinda stuff. See, if I only coulda gotten that moron's name.
VIVIAN: Well, Peter, "If at first you don't succeed..."

PETER: Yeah, yeah, yeah.
STAN: "Yeah, yeah, yeah." Sit down and eat!
　(Peter sits quickly and begins to dig into his food. Stan starts
　eating as Vivian looks between Peter and Stan, then...)
VIVIAN: Stanley, when you finish eatin', you could show Peter
　your rock collection.
PETER: He doesn't have to. I saw 'em already. They're nice.
VIVIAN: Him and Scott found 'em up on Garret Mountain.
PETER: Oh, really. How very interesting.
VIVIAN: Most of 'em are quartz.
PETER: Wow. (Pause)
VIVIAN: Stanley says there's a lota quartz around here.
PETER: Oh, really. How very interesting.
VIVIAN: Most of the country is quartz. Right, Stanley?
PETER: That's great.
VIVIAN: Tell Peter what ya used to tell Scott, Stanley.
PETER: He doesn't have to.
STAN: About what?
VIVIAN: About how it's good to know about rocks.
STAN: I'm eatin' here.
VIVIAN: Go ahead, Stanley.
PETER: Oh yes Stanley, please do.
STAN: I used to tell 'im how it's good to know about rocks. What
　kinda rocks ya live on.
PETER: What do you mean?
STAN: (Taps bat on floor) What's down there, in the ground.
PETER: What for?
STAN: Because the more we know about the things around us, the
　more we know about ourselves.
VIVIAN: Isn't that nice?
PETER: Yeah, but what does that have to do with rocks?
VIVIAN: Tell 'im, Stanley.
STAN: Rocks are something around us. Rocks are in the dirt.
PETER: Yeah.
STAN: And the dirt is what we'd stand on, if we didn't have
　floors.

PETER: So what does that have to do with anything?

STAN: Well, it's always good to know where ya stand.

VIVIAN: Stanley says that when he goes outside, he could tell what kinda rock is under him...just by standin' on it. (Pause) Tell Peter what ya told me about dirt, Stanley.

STAN: I don't want to.

VIVIAN: Go ahead, Stanley.

PETER: Yeah, Stanley. Go on, tell me about the dirt.

VIVIAN: Go on, Stanley.

STAN: Alright. Alright. (Pause) The way I figure it, history is all the dirt...and the different times piled on top of one another. Like layers. And the time we're livin' on now...we're just one pile of dirt...one layer of dirt in the history of things...and we're on top for now...living "on top of the world." But someday, we'll be packed in, one on top of the other...with all the other layers...and all the other times.

VIVIAN: (After a pause) Isn't that nice?

PETER: I don't know. I just think there's something bad about it, that's all.

STAN: What?

PETER: History.

STAN: What's bad about it?

PETER: I don't know. Just the idea of caring about something in the past tense so much. I mean what's the point of caring about something that isn't now? Like today. There was no history in the day I lived today. Nobody was living in the past, everybody was right there... where they were... in the present. And that's how I feel so much sometimes I could just explode, ya know?

VIVIAN: What do ya mean "explode," Peter?

PETER: I mean every time I get in front of a group of people, I realize that what I'm talkin' about...all that is "now," see? Like me, I'm "now." I'm not "then," or in the past.

STAN: Aha! There, see...ya can't have a "now" without a "then."

PETER: Yeah, but what's the use of a "then" for instance, Stan, when the "now" of somethin' sucks so much? Sorry, Vivian.

STAN: Well, "now" never "sucks" so much, if ya learn somethin'
from back then.
VIVIAN: Oh, boy, isn't this --
PETER: -- look, I'm not sayin' history is stupid, Stan. I'm just
sayin' it doesn't apply.
STAN: We are "living history."
PETER: We are living "now," Stan. We are living in Passaic,
New Jersey..."now." I need a briefcase.
STAN: A briefcase?
PETER: Yeah, a black one with gold latches and my initials on it.
One of the kind that you could put on your lap and flip it open
with one snap of your thumb. I saw some hot ass guy on the bus
today with one of 'em.
STAN: And what are you gonna put in your briefcase?
PETER: Everything I have.
STAN: And what is that?
VIVIAN: Stanley.
PETER: You know, my books. And I'll make xerox copies and
draw some kinda charts and stuff to show people. Plus pens and
stuff.
VIVIAN: There's a luggage place in Clifton.
PETER: I have to get it in the city.
STAN: Why?
PETER: Because it's more expensive there. See, ya get a
briefcase...and they kind of protect ya. It's kinda like armor or
somethin', or one of those...what do ya call those things that
knights have. You know, like in *Robin Hood* and stuff?
STAN: A lance?
PETER: Yeah, that's all I need is one of those.
STAN: You need a lance?
PETER: No, a briefcase. See, a briefcase is a kind of "mental
lance." See, that was my problem today, that I didn't have one
of those. Ya take one of those knight's lances away... and he's
a sitting duck. He's a dead man. (Pause) Now, could we all just
take a little time here to eat? I'm starvin', and I can't eat, talk
and think at the same time.

VIVIAN: Oh, yeah. Go ahead and eat, Stanley.

(Peter finally sits and begins to eat. Stan slowly gets up, makes his way across the kitchen, turns to Peter)

STAN: Where are you from again, Peter Hogancamp?

VIVIAN: Stanley.

PETER: (With mouth full) What do ya mean?

STAN: Which part of town?

VIVIAN: Stanley.

PETER: I told ya. State Street.

STAN: Well, when's the last time you were there?

PETER: The last time I had to be.

STAN: Well, you oughta go back again. You oughta do research on yourself.

VIVIAN: Stanley --

PETER: -- there isn't anything there.

STAN: There is to you.

PETER: What are you talkin' about?

STAN: History.

PETER: I told ya, everybody's dead.

VIVIAN: Stanley.

STAN: What?

VIVIAN: Peter, honey, take Kelly for a walk.

(Peter gets up, goes to the wall and takes Kelly's leash, which is hanging on a nail)

PETER: Alright, alright.

(Peter opens the door, but turns around first, grabbing a roll off the table. He exits, slamming the door behind him. Vivian and Stan are alone)

VIVIAN: Don't make any trouble, Stanley. (Pause) Don't make any trouble.

(The lights fade slowly to black)

Act One, Scene Three

> (As the lights come up the next day, we see Stan and Peter
> coming into the kitchen from the outside. Vivian is there to
> greet them)

VIVIAN: Here they are...the rock explorers!

STAN: He's no explorer.

PETER: Don't start, Stan.

VIVIAN: Did ya find any rocks?

STAN: They're not rocks!

> (Peter holds up what appear to be two small black rocks)

PETER: Yeah, we got some rocks.

STAN: They're not rocks for Christ sake.

VIVIAN: Stan...

STAN: We weren't even up there for five minutes.

PETER: We were up there for five minutes, Stan.

STAN: You're supposed to follow the vein...you're supposed to
dig.

PETER: We did dig.

STAN: We did not.

> (Peter holds up the "rocks")

PETER: Then what do ya call these, Stan?

STAN: They're pieces of asphalt for Christ sake.

PETER: They are not, they're rocks.

STAN: They're pieces of the road for Christ sake. Smell 'em.

> (Peter smells the "rocks")

PETER: They smell like rocks to me. What's the matter with
'em?

STAN: Forget it.

VIVIAN: How long were ya up there, Peter?

PETER: Long enough to find rocks.

STAN: They're pieces of the road for--

PETER: -- hey, look! I'm not gonna shoot off my scientific wad of knowledge right here, but I did go to high school for three and one half years, and I do know enough about rocks to know when I'm holdin' one in my hand. And what I have in my hand right now is nothing but pure rock.

STAN: Then why do they smell like tar?

PETER: Because... why do ya think? What do ya think? Tar is at the bottom of the earth, where all the dinosaurs are, right? That's what all the dinosaurs turned into; oil and tar! These are all commonly known facts of the dinosauric age, okay? This is all grade school stuff. And what do we know for a fact the center of the earth is made of? Hard tar. And what does hard tar look like when it comes to the surface? Black rocks... like these... in my hand.

STAN: So dinosaurs turned into tar?

PETER: I didn't say that. I said... I didn't say... see now you're... (Looks to Vivian)... see what he does? The reason they're... the dinosaurs were... they fell into tar pits, and they got stuck in 'em, and they just stayed there, because who can help a huge friggin' dinosaur... they're the biggest things on earth, okay? So they just stood there, trapped in the tar pits, sad and disappointed like that until eventually they starved to death because they couldn't get any food. That's how all the... and then when they all died, they sank to the bottom. And then time and erosion took over, and they were covered up with everything thats happened since... so that even though they died on what *seemed* to them to be the top of the earth... by the time "now" came along... all the earth got squished down to the bottom of it. And since the center of the earth is so hot... everything melted and became... tar. (Peter holds the "rocks" up ceremoniously) And these rocks, are the ancient remnants of that! (Pause)

STAN: They're pieces of the road, for Christ sake.

(Stan slowly turns around and goes into the house)

VIVIAN: Did ya really try to look for rocks, Peter?

PETER: Yeah, what do ya think? Yeah. (Peter smells the rocks) Well, I gotta catch the bus into the city. I wanna drop off some of those letters.

VIVIAN: I picked up some of those envelopes you wanted Peter. I put 'em in your briefcase.

PETER: Thanks, Vivian. (Pause. Peter takes his briefcase and heads for the door, stops, turns to Vivian) Look, Vivian, I really did try. I really did try to look for stuff, but the mountain isn't the same I don't think. It's not even really a mountain anymore.

VIVIAN: What do ya mean?

PETER: I mean I drove up there...like he told me, but they're blastin' it all out. Even the ledge where everybody used to park...it's not there anymore. It's not like --

VIVIAN: -- what are they doin'?

PETER: They're puttin' up condos...you know, leveling it all out, so most of the roads up there were blocked off. "Overview Mansions" they're gonna call 'em. I didn't tell, Stan. I mean he asked me what all the noise was, but I told 'im they were just fixin' the road or somethin'. I thought that was in keeping with his not knowing his dog was dead.

VIVIAN: Thank you, Peter.

(Peter again heads for the door, turns again)

PETER: I mean I'm not sayin' I did the best I could, but ya can't expect me to just pick up rock collecting like that. I mean however much of a stupid thing it might sound like, it's still a science, and ya can't just...I mean Scott should take him, not me. It's a father son thing to do, not a whatever I am to Stan thing to do.

VIVIAN: Don't worry about it, Peter, I won't ask ya to go with 'im anymore.

PETER: Okay. (Peter heads toward the door again, turns back) Do you think it's true about...you know, people who lose one thing, make it up with another?

VIVIAN: What do ya mean?

PETER: I mean...on our way down what was left of the mountain, Stan started tellin' me which way to go. You know, like he could see where he was goin'.

VIVIAN: Well, he can. Stanley has his own way of seein' things...without his eyes.

PETER: But I mean, he didn't take me back here. He started tellin' me to just make a left here, and then a right here, and before I knew it, he had us on State Street headin' toward Mortimer.

VIVIAN: What's down there?

PETER: State and Mortimer...on the corner.

VIVIAN: What's that?

PETER: Then he told me to pull it over and park it, and he pointed with his finger across my nose, and I turned and looked over...and I couldn't believe it.

VIVIAN: What?

PETER: He took me all the way through Passaic, and without my even knowin' it, had me park the car across the street from the house I grew up in...all my life...or at least until I left.

VIVIAN: Isn't that funny?

PETER: Well...actually, no, it isn't. I mean I never...I just told 'im...I mean I thought I just said I lived down on the end of State...but how did he know which house?

VIVIAN: Stanley is just...he's a historian, that's all.

PETER: Yeah, but --

VIVIAN: -- so does it look the same?

PETER: Yeah. Pretty much. Except it used to be white. (Pause) I don't know why he took me there. If I wanted to see it, I woulda taken the ten minute walk myself.

VIVIAN: Oh, don't make a big to-do about it, honey.

PETER: Christ, I haven't been back there in like fifteen years.

VIVIAN: Well, now you don't have to go back for another fifteen.

PETER: Yeah, I guess.

(Pause. Peter takes out one of his father's old books, holds it)

PETER: It's where he brought all his associates back...you know, after he had to make a speech somewhere. I used to listen to 'em all talkin' while I was sittin' at the top of the stairs. All the top heads from everywhere...all the biggest clubs and associations in New Jersey. Or at least in the town anyway. Kiwanis, Elks, Rotary, all the big ones. And my father was the MC at everything they ever did.

VIVIAN: Wow, that's somethin'. (Pause) Are ya' hungry, Peter?

PETER: No, no, that's okay. (Pause) Anyway, just for the hell of it I checked out the place a little bit.

VIVIAN: Oh, yeah?

PETER: Yeah. You know, it's the same old place really. All in all though, it's just a house no matter how ya look at it.

VIVIAN: Sure, that's all it is.

PETER: Ya know what the weird thing was though, Vivian?

VIVIAN: What? (Pause)

PETER: I was walkin' up the stairs...out in front...and I looked at myself from the outside...you know, like objective. And it was weird. I looked more like my father when I looked at myself...then I looked like me. Or at least the way I looked the last time I was there. I was just a kid.

VIVIAN: Well, that's normal, Peter, everybody is different from the way they were. Now, why don't ya go inside and make up with Stanley?

PETER: It was like a homecoming or somethin' for two different people, but only one of 'em showed up... because the other one was dead. But that didn't matter, because the person who was there... was as much the person who wasn't... as he was himself. (Pause) Do ya know what I mean, Vivian? What is that?

VIVIAN: You're just tired, Peter, from all your business. Now sit down and rest your feet.

PETER: I don't want to sit down, Vivian. See, it's weird how one thing you remember can make you remember somethin' else...like the stairs...and Mrs. Beasley, remember?

VIVIAN: Who's Mrs. Beasley?

PETER: On *Family Affair*, that stupid show with Mr. French and everything...and Buffy...and... I don't remember the other kid's name... Jody or somethin'.

VIVIAN: Oh, yeah.

PETER: Well, Mrs. Beasley was Buffy's doll...only I never knew that. I just kept thinkin' Mrs. Beasley was like a normal person...like a teacher...Buffy's teacher or somethin'.

VIVIAN: Yeah.

PETER: And so that's when I remembered myself on the stairs again...not the time with all the K of C guys, but the time when I heard my father...he was cryin'.

VIVIAN: Cryin'?

PETER: Yeah. I wasn't sure when I heard it at first, so I just sat on top of the stairs for awhile. And then I heard it. He was cryin'. So I went downstairs, and he was watchin' *Family Affair*.

(Stan appears in the doorway leading to the house, out of sight of Peter and Vivian. He remains there in silhouette, unseen)

VIVIAN: Is that why he was cryin'?

PETER: I don't think so, but that's what I thought too...that somebody died on it or somethin'. So I just sat there next to 'im and I go, "Hey dad, how come you're cryin'?" And he didn't say anything. So I just sat there next to 'im...watchin' it with 'im and that's where I remember findin' out Mrs. Beasley was a doll. I was only like ten or somethin'. (Pause) Then I heard the click.

VIVIAN: Click?

PETER: Yeah, my father had a gun in his mouth, and his hand was in his mouth --

VIVIAN: -- Peter --

PETER: -- and then "pow" --

VIVIAN: -- oh, my God, Peter --

PETER: -- and then "ping." (Pause) He missed.

VIVIAN: What?

PETER: He missed. He had the gun in his mouth...and he pulled the trigger...and he missed. Don't ask me how a guy could miss...when he had a gun in his hand...and his hand was in his mouth...but he did. He missed. That was the "ping." He shot my mother's souvenir liberty bell behind 'im. (Pause) God, that was the weirdest fuckin' thing.

VIVIAN: Peter, honey --

PETER: -- and then I remember not wantin' him to feel any worse, so I just sat there...and I kept pretendin' like I was watchin' *Family Affair*...and he kept cryin' for awhile... and then he went back into the kitchen... and then he came out with a band aid on his head.

VIVIAN: Peter --

PETER: -- he must've skimmed his head with the bullet. (Pause) Well, if you're not gonna do it one way -- you're gonna do it another. So what was I...see, there it goes again.

VIVIAN: What?

PETER: See, even though he ended up dyin' of somethin' other than himself, what killed him was his state of mind. See, that's how my father died, Vivian. He killed himself without his havin' to do it, that's all, and I'm not gonna do that. I'm not gonna let that happen to me. I'm gonna run and talk so fast through this life that nothin's gonna catch me...least of all myself...

VIVIAN: -- well, that's fine, Peter, now --

PETER: -- just keep on talkin', that's all. The faster I talk the less anybody knows what the fuck I'm talkin' about....and the more they think I'm sayin' somethin' smart. But ya can't be scared of the world. He was scared of the --

VIVIAN: -- now, Peter, calm down. Don't --

(Stan disappears in the doorway)

PETER: -- all I wanna be is not be like him. My father was a "done to" not a "doer." He let life do more to him than he did to it. And I don't wanna do that --

VIVIAN: -- Peter --

PETER: -- ya can't be scared of the world, Vivian. All ya gotta
do is keep runnin'...even faster than history if you have to --
VIVIAN: -- Peter --
PETER: I can run even faster than history --
VIVIAN: -- Peter --
PETER: -- maybe I can, Vivian. Maybe *I* can! (Peter collects
himself, looks at Vivian) See, what...see what happens...my
head goes in all...where's my briefcase, Vivian?
VIVIAN: It's in your hand, honey.
PETER: Oh. Yeah.
VIVIAN: Peter, you're gonna miss your bus.
PETER: Yeah. Well, it's too late now I guess.
VIVIAN: You can go tomorrow.
PETER: Yeah.
(Peter stands in the middle of the kitchen, still)
VIVIAN: Peter? Peter, honey, do ya want somethin' to eat?
PETER: Stan shouldn't of taken me back, Vivian. He shouldn't
have taken me back.

(Vivian watches Peter as the lights fade slowly to black)

Act Two, Scene One

(As lights come up, we see Stan sitting at the table listening
to a baseball game on a transistor radio. There's a can
of beer on the table. Peter enters through the outside door
in a hurry, carrying his briefcase)

PETER: Stan!
STAN: Here he is.
PETER: Anybody call, Stan?
STAN: Nobody called.
(Peter checks the dial tone on the phone)
PETER: Where's Vivian?
STAN: She went shoppin'.

PETER: Shit -- what if somebody calls? Stan, if somebody calls, you're gonna have to help me out.

STAN: Hey...I ain't gonna do nothin'. Now just settle down and stop buzzin' around me here.

(Peter goes to the fridge, grabs a beer. He sits across from Stan. Stan doesn't like what he's hearing about the game. He turns it off. Peter and Stan sit there, for awhile, awkwardly. Finally, Peter looks toward Stan's bat)

PETER: You like baseball, don't ya, Stan?

STAN: Boy, you're a regular detective, aren't ya?

PETER: That's a real Louisville Slugger ya got there, isn't it?

STAN: Yeah, what about it?

PETER: Nothin', I was just wonderin'. I mean ya don't see wood around much, that's all. Everything is mostly aluminum nowadays. Where'd ya get it?

STAN: (Pause) I got it for the kid.

PETER: I used to play ya know.

STAN: You?

PETER: Yeah, me. What's so hard to believe about that?

STAN: Well...everything.

PETER: (Gets up) Let me see it, Stan.

STAN: What?

PETER: The bat, let me see it. (Stan slowly hands the bat to Peter. Peter sets, as though at bat) Three and two, Stan, two outs, bases loaded, bottom of the sixth. We only played six innings in little league, so the bottom of the sixth is like the ninth anywhere else. It was now or never for little "Petey" Hogancamp... the day he was gonna finally make his mark on the world. Bobby Walton on the mound, best pitcher in Passaic, and me standin' at the plate thinkin' I could never do it, I could never do it... and then it came to me.

STAN: What?

PETER: The fact that maybe, just maybe, Stan, I could. So I step outa the box a second and I reassess my situation. I'm only twelve, Stan, and already I'm reassessing my situations. And it comes to me that I'm bigger than my fear and that I'm bigger

PETER: (Cont) than this bat and I'm bigger than the ball that
    Bobby Walton is about to whip at me right now...and so I step
    into the box again and Bobby starts his wind-up...and
    everything in the field gets quiet...like in a church...and then I
    remember seeing him release it...it's a strike, right down the
    pipe and it's as big as a watermelon, and I could feel my arms
    come around in what felt like slow motion...and then I swung
    what had to be the most perfect swing in the history of The
    Passaic Little League...and by the time my swing was over
    Stan, I knew that I had become the maker of my own fate, and
    that now I could do anything...and that nothing...*nothing* could
    stand in my way.
STAN: (After a pause) So what happened?
PETER: What I just said, Stan. I had a beatific vision about the
    size of myself in relation to my fears. I conquered my worst
    enemy; the self in me that doubted the self in me that...
STAN: --ya struck out, didn't ya?
PETER: --okay, in a "pragmatic" sense, yeah, I "struck out." But
    what I gained in my head by striking out is unmeasurable.
    Better to hit a home run in yourself mentally, Stan, than to hit
    a home run in some stupid little, little league game in Passaic,
    New Jersey. What about you?
STAN: What about me?
PETER: Did you play?
STAN: Oh, yeah. I played in the service. I hit more home runs
    over the fence back then than I did in my head though.
PETER: Oh yeah? Well, what do ya think of this...Stanley? Ted
    Williams was the greatest baseball player that ever lived.
STAN: That's right.
PETER: What?
STAN: I said -- that's right.
PETER: Are you agreeing with me?
STAN : Yup.
PETER: Holy shit.
STAN: Sweetest swing in the game.
PETER: Ever see 'im play?

STAN: Sure, when I did jobs up in Boston.
PETER: You a Bosox fan?
STAN: Always have been.
PETER: This is scary, Stan. We agree on two things.
STAN: (After a pause) Well, it was bound to happen sooner or later.
(Peter stands, checks the dial tone on phone, turns to Stan)
PETER: Well, why don't we...I mean I know somebody at the Y who gets tickets real cheap and the Sox are comin' into Yankee Stadium in a couple of weeks so...I mean I'm not askin' or anything, but if you wanna...I would...I mean if you wanna go to a game I would, but I'm not asking or anything. It's up to you.
STAN: Yeah. Yeah, sure. I guess we could do that.
(Vivian enters with groceries)
VIVIAN: Peter! Did ya get the job?
PETER: (Taking the bags) Vivian, how many times do I have to tell you about that, huh?
VIVIAN: Oh. Yeah, yeah.
(Peter puts the bags on the counter and runs to his briefcase. He picks it up, opens it)
PETER: Voila! (Peter shows Vivian the inside of the briefcase) What do ya see, Vivian?
VIVIAN: Nothin'.
PETER: That's right. That's because they're all out there. All my letter portfolio proposal things. "I'm" out there. I hit like seventeen places today, and I don't feel like I could say one of 'em was anti-receptive to me. In every place I went, they all took my letter, and two of 'em even let me see the seminar rooms.
STAN: Where are these places?
PETER: Where do ya think, Stan? New York, New York.
VIVIAN: Are they nice, Peter?
PETER: Well, that's the thing. I mean I coulda gone to the top scale places that I checked out...you know, Sheraton and the Hiltons and all that, but instead I took a step down on the scale

PETER: (Cont) a little and hit more...mid-level places. You
    know, all still good and everything...all still in New York...but
    a little more...mid-scale...a little more...intimate.
STAN: Like where?
PETER: You know...Best Westerns...Howard Johnson's...
VIVIAN: Oh.
PETER: But New York is New York. It's better to do a Best
    Western in New York than a Sheraton in Secaucus, I don't care
    what anybody says. And I'll tell ya, the more time I spend
    standin' on the street next to big buildings...the less I feel so
    small standin' next to 'em. And that's the way I felt in there
    today...not so small anymore.
STAN: What's so small?
PETER: What?
STAN: What's so small over here?
PETER: Nothin' Stan, that's not what I'm talkin' about. What's
    big or small isn't "it"...or what something "is," it's how ya see
    "it"...or how you see what "it" is.
STAN: What is "it?" What are you talkin' about?
PETER: I'm talkin' about perception, Stan... not what people
    see...but how they see it. Like you and me and history. How
    you see it one way and I see it another. Or like rock collecting
    or the ground, or whatever. I'll tell ya what, Stan, I'll give ya
    a history lesson in perception, okay? (Peter goes to stand in the
    middle of the kitchen floor, pushing the kitchen table and some
    of the chairs out of the way. He finds one particular place on the
    floor, surveys it, then looks back to Stan) Now, if I were
    standing on the ground right now instead of the floor, I would
    be as far away from the earth as I am tall... right? So, since I'm
    around six feet... I'm six feet away from the earth. But, if I
    knelt down like this... (Peter kneels on the floor) ...I'd cut my
    relationship to the earth in half. Now I'm three feet away from
    the earth... from all the rocks... and from all your history, and
    from all your crap like that. Do ya follow me so far, Stan?
STAN: Not really.

PETER: Now, if I got down on my face, like this….(Peter lies on the floor, face down) …I'd be as close to the earth as I could get…without bein' in it. (Pause) So. (Pause) Soooooooooo. (Pause)

STAN: Yeah?

PETER: What was my point?

STAN: That's what I'd like to know!

    (A longish pause. Awkward silence as Peter remains still, head to the ground)

VIVIAN: Well…there isn't any rush, honey. Why don't you think about it for awhile. Do you want me to bring your beer down there for ya?

PETER: Vivian…

    (Stan pounds his bat into the floor, Peter jumps up)

STAN: *This* is the earth!?

PETER: Yeah.

STAN: You're talkin' about…how close you are to the earth?

PETER: Yeah.

STAN: See, that's it. Right there.

PETER: What?

STAN: When you're lyin' on the ground, there is no difference between you and the dirt.

PETER: What are you talkin' about?

STAN: Because…like the dinosaurs…after they all died…now they're all dirt…and that's what you are… but you just don't know it yet…because you aren't it yet.

PETER: I'm not what yet?

STAN: The dirt.

PETER: I'm not the dirt yet.

STAN: That's right. But you will be.

PETER: And I'll be the dinosaurs, too…right, Stanley?

STAN: That's right. Everybody will be. See, you don't get it now, and Scott didn't get it before ya. This is what you gotta understand; No matter how tall anybody is… or how close they are to the ground… everybody's the same size someday… and a million years after. And so is Passaic. There is no difference

STAN: (Cont) between the size of the buildings over there and over here, because someday they're all gonna be just like the dinosaurs, too.

PETER: Passaic is gonna be just like the dinosaurs, too.

STAN: That's right. (Pause)

PETER: And all that...what you just said, Stan...that doesn't sound a little bit uh, well, stupid to you at all?

(Vivian moves to recorder)

VIVIAN: Peter, honey--

PETER: -- 'cause I can't talk for anybody else but me, Stan, but as far as I know, I'm not the dinosaurs. I'm Peter Hogancamp.

VIVIAN: Peter --

(Vivian presses the recorder. We hear Kelly bark once or twice as the phone rings. Vivian stops Kelly barking as Peter turns to the phone)

PETER: Holy shit!

STAN: What? (Ring)

PETER: This is it!

STAN: Hey, what's goin' on here!?

(Ring. Vivian moves to answer it)

PETER: Vivian, do you remember what I said?

VIVIAN: About what?

PETER: The phone...remember? (Ring)

STAN: Hey, get the --

VIVIAN: -- oh.

PETER: Say it!

VIVIAN: (Ring) Oh, Peter, do I have to?

PETER: Vivian, please!

(Peter places the ringing phone right in front of Vivian. Vivian picks it up)

VIVIAN: Hogan...Hogancamp entrepre...entrepre...

PETER: (Quick, to Vivian) -- entrepreneurial!

VIVIAN: (In phone) -- entrepr...entre --

PETER: (Quick) -- entrepreneurial!

VIVIAN: -- entre...entre --

PETER: -- enterprises! Enterprises!

STAN: Hey, what are ya....
PETER: (Quick, to Stan) Shh!
VIVIAN: Enterprises. Hello.
PETER: (Under his breath) Shit.
STAN: (To Peter) What is that? What are you...
PETER: Shh!
VIVIAN: (In phone) Yes, he's here. "Hold please." (Vivian hands
  Peter the phone) Peter, it's for you.
PETER: No! (Peter panics, runs into the broom closet, slams the
  door to simulate his "other" office, then comes right out)
  Alright, Mrs. Merkel...I'll take it in this office!
STAN: What office?
PETER: (To Stan) Shh! (Peter takes the phone, speaks into it)
  Hogancamp. Right.... right. Oh, of course, Mr. Kinghorn...
  yes... oh great, right, well let me check my days here. I think
  that's within the realm of feasibility. Hm, Thursday, Thursday,
  Thursday, oh, here's a clear one... but wait... let me check...
  (Peter calls to Vivian) Mrs. Merkel, do we know about
  Stamford on the 14th yet?
VIVIAN: What?
PETER: (Shaking his head "no") Stamford. Is that still on next
  week?
VIVIAN: (In a panic) I --
PETER: -- great! (In the phone) That's fine. Great... great...
  great... alrighty. Good talkin' to ya, Mr. Kinghorn. Righto...
  bye bye now. (Peter hangs up) Holy shit. I'm not home ten
  minutes and the phones are ringin' off the hook.
VIVIAN: Who was it?
PETER: A hotel.
STAN: In New York?
PETER: Where do ya think?
VIVIAN: Are they gonna hire ya?
PETER: Vivian...
STAN: Are they gonna pay ya?
PETER: Yeah...yeah. (Pause) After awhile.

STAN: What does that mean?

PETER: I gotta demonstrate first. You know, give a sample course.

VIVIAN: Is it a big place?

PETER: Oh, yeah. It's right across from a Hilton.

VIVIAN: (To Stan) A Hilton.

STAN: What's the name of it?

PETER: (After a pause) The Peter Pan.

STAN: The Peter Pan. I never heard of that.

PETER: It's got a good room for seminars.

VIVIAN: Well, that's somethin'.

PETER: Yeah, but it's more than just that. Anyway, it's not where I'm doin' it...but where the place is that I'm doin' it in. It's in the city.

VIVIAN: That's right.

PETER: I'm ahead of him. How many offers do ya think my father got from over there?

VIVIAN: How many?

STAN: How do ya figure you got an offer if ya don't even know ya got the job yet?

PETER: "Inquiries" then, Stan. What's the difference? Guess how many?

VIVIAN: How many?

PETER: None. See, already I'm ahead of 'im. See what happens when ya open yourself up to the full scope of possibilities?

STAN: Here he goes again.

VIVIAN: Stanley...

(Peter grabs his briefcase)

PETER: Don't worry about it, Stan. Don't worry about sayin' anything wrong to me anymore. Because I'm not here anymore.

STAN: What is he talkin' about?

PETER: You could say anything you want to me now, Stan. Because I already got one "mental foot" outside that door.

STAN: What mental foot?

PETER: It's only my physical body that's here now, Stan.
Everything else is on its way out already... floatin' over The
Passaic... and then over The Hudson... and then someday over
the whole friggin' ocean. And once ya get yourself to the point
where I am now...where you could float over everything ya
ever felt was keepin' you down... then you could go anywhere. (Pause) When I get this thing, Stan, I'll buy you all
the rocks you want.

STAN: Ya can't buy rocks.

PETER: ...quartz, concrete, whatever kind ya want.

STAN: YA CAN'T BUY ROCKS!

VIVIAN: Peter...

PETER: What?

VIVIAN: Kelly.

(Peter goes toward the door, handing his briefcase over to
Vivian)

PETER: Thanks, Vivian...I mean for --

VIVIAN: -- that's alright, honey. (Peter exits. Vivian turns to
Stan) Stanley, he's tryin'. Give him a chance.

STAN: I'm tryin' to give him a chance. He's another talker, I told
ya.

VIVIAN: Look, Stanley, he got a call.

STAN: So, he got a call. (Pause) Nobody calls us.

VIVIAN: No, nobody calls us. (Pause) But maybe somebody
would, Stanley. Maybe if you would call Scott...

STAN: --Hey--

VIVIAN: --I just think---

STAN: I don't wanna talk about him.

VIVIAN: I'm only thinkin', Stanley, that's all...

STAN: I said, I DON'T WANNA TALK ABOUT HIM!

(Vivian glares at Stan)

VIVIAN: Alright, Stanley. But give *Peter* a chance. Who knows?
Maybe he'll surprise ya.

(Stan turns away, Vivian looks toward him as the lights fade to
black)

Act Two, Scene Two

(As the lights come up, we see Peter sitting in the kitchen, motionless. Soon after, Vivian enters in a nightdress)

VIVIAN: Peter? (No response) Peter?

PETER: Oh, Vivian. Sorry. Did I wake you up or somethin'?

VIVIAN: No. No, honey. What are you doin' up so late? Tomorrow's your big day.

PETER: Yeah, I know. I...I couldn't get to sleep, that's all.

VIVIAN: Are you alright?

PETER: Oh, yeah. Yeah. I'm okay.

VIVIAN: Well, do ya want some milk or somethin'?

PETER: No, that's okay. I'm just sittin' here thinkin'.

VIVIAN: Well, do ya want me to stay up with ya?

PETER: No, Vivian. I'm okay. I'm not a kid anymore...I don't need my "milky" before bedtime.

VIVIAN: Alright, honey. I was just askin'. (Vivian turns to leave) Turn off the lights when ya come up.

PETER: Yeah, sure. (Vivian exits. Peter sits alone a moment, uneasy. Suddenly he sprints off his chair and runs after her, whispering loudly) Vivian?

VIVIAN: (Entering) What honey?

PETER: Nothin', I was just...I was just thinking that if you were gonna have some milk, then I would too. I mean if you want it -- I don't want to deny you it.

VIVIAN: Okay.

(Vivian goes to get the milk)

PETER: Nobody else called, Vivian. I put seventeen proposals out and in a whole week I only get one call?

VIVIAN: Well, one is better than none.

PETER: Yeah, but it's awfully close to none, Vivian. I need this thing. I mean it's not exactly like I have a plan "B" right now.

VIVIAN: You'll get it, Peter. You'll get it. Just have a little patience, that's all.

(Vivian hands Peter the milk)

PETER: Thanks. (Vivian sits) Vivian, could I tell you somethin'
  You know...confidential?
VIVIAN: Sure, honey.
PETER: I was walkin' in the tunnel today, Vivian.
VIVIAN: What?
PETER: I was walkin' in The Lincoln Tunnel. Right down the
  middle of it. But you're not supposed to. It's illegal.
VIVIAN: Well, what do ya mean, in a dream or somethin'?
PETER: Well, no, see that's the problem.
  (Peter removes a piece of paper from his pocket)
VIVIAN: (Takes it) What is this?
PETER: It's a ticket. I got a ticket for walkin' through the tunnel.
  See it says "jaywalking" on it because the cops couldn't figure
  out what else to call it.
VIVIAN: Peter, you coulda killed yourself.
PETER: I had to, Vivian.
VIVIAN: Why?
PETER: Because...alright, now, Vivian, don't look at me funny
  when I tell you this, alright?
VIVIAN: What?
PETER: I saw a ghost.
VIVIAN: What?
PETER: In the city, when I was at the bus station today... a ghost
  came up to me. Don't look at me funny, Vivian. A ghost came
  up to me, only he was disguised as a bum. He came up to me,
  just like any other bum, but he didn't ask me for a quarter. He
  came up to me and he said: "Get your ass home. Your father's
  waitin' for ya. Your father's waitin' for ya," he said.
VIVIAN: Peter, that place is fulla crazies.
PETER: No, wait. Wait. So I told 'im: "My father's dead. My
  father is dead." And that's when I knew there was somethin'
  scary goin' on. Because in one blink of an eye he was
  gone...and there was nothin' else there --
VIVIAN: -- Peter --
PETER: -- wait! And there was nothin' else there except for the
  smell of Lucky Strikes. And Vivian --

VIVIAN: -- Peter, there's a million --
PETER: -- and the reason I know for sure that there's somethin'
true about what happened is --
VIVIAN: -- because your father smoked 'em.
PETER: That's right.
VIVIAN: Honey, ya can't put any meaning in somethin' like that.
PETER: (After a pause) So anyway, I start runnin' to the ticket
place, you know to get a bus out, but there isn't one for another hour, so I figure what the hell, so I walk down the ramp
really calm and slow, and I walk right into the tunnel. And I
get about a football field in before I start hearin' sirens... and
then I get all discombobulated... because when ya get all turned
around in a tunnel, ya can't tell which way you came from, or
which way you're goin', because both ways look exactly the
same. And all this time the cars are whizzin' by me and I'm
thinkin' "go ahead and hit me... go ahead and hit me, you
bastards." Because nothin's gonna hurt me --
VIVIAN: -- Peter --
PETER: -- nothin's gonna hurt me. I got my briefcase right? And
that's all I need. See as long as I have that --
VIVIAN: -- Peter --
PETER: -- see, as long as I have my briefcase...
VIVIAN: -- Peter, honey, drink your milk.
(Vivian gets up and stands behind Peter, calming him with her
presence)
PETER: Okay. (Pause) Okay, Vivian. Thanks.
VIVIAN: Well...how much is the ticket for?
PETER: Oh, yeah. Well, jaywalking is usually fifteen bucks. But
he added another fifteen because it was in a tunnel. And I guess
he figured...
VIVIAN: Well, that ain't bad.
(Vivian walks over to her purse, takes out thirty dollars and
quietly slides it toward Peter)
PETER: Thanks. (Pause) And listen, Vivian, do me a favor and
don't tell Stan about, you know, whatever it was I saw today.
VIVIAN: I won't, honey.

PETER: Okay, thanks. (Pause, Peter gets up) Well, listen, I don't
wanna keep you up or anything.
VIVIAN: Oh, you're not keepin' me up. I'm always up at
night...takin' walks around the house.
PETER: What?
VIVIAN: Oh, I just like to putz around the house sometimes. It's
the only time I could, when Stanley is in bed.
PETER: You take walks around your house?
VIVIAN: Oh, I know it's silly. But I just like to walk around...
lookin' at things.
PETER: What things? What is there to look at in a kitchen? You
have to expand your mental horizons, Vivian.
VIVIAN: Oh, I know. I know. I just like lookin' at little things.
PETER: Like what?
VIVIAN: Well. Anything. (Vivian quickly looks around, finally
settling her eyes on Peter's glass) Look, right now I'm lookin'
at somethin'.
PETER: What?
VIVIAN: Your glass.
PETER: What about it?
VIVIAN: Do ya see what's on it?
PETER: (Looking at glass) What is it...a clown or somethin'?
VIVIAN: It's Ronald McDonald.
PETER: Oh. Oh, yeah. So?
VIVIAN: Well, that's only *one* thing I saw.
PETER: So what makes it so worth seeing?
VIVIAN: Well. I look at it...and I see...Scott. And he's ten. And
I see Stanley. And we're all driving down to Florida to see
Stanley's brother, Herman. And Scott is hanging out the
window, and Stanley is tellin' 'im, "Get your head in the car!"
And Scott yells out, "Dad, McDonald's! Dad, McDonald's!"
And Stanley looks at me, and he smiles. And I shake my head
"Okay," and...well...
PETER: What?

VIVIAN: Oh, I wish I could talk like you and Stanley, about "history" and "dinosaurs" and stuff like that. But that's what I see when I see that glass.
(Peter looks at glass)
PETER: God.
VIVIAN: See, that's kinda like seeing ghosts, too. Isn't it? (Pause) All my life I always think someday I'm gonna win the lottery and take everybody on a trip around the world.
PETER: Well, ya still could, Vivian.
VIVIAN: Oh, it doesn't matter anymore.
PETER: What do you mean, it matters! Everything ya want matters. It's just a matter of widening your mental horizons, that's all.
VIVIAN: Well, it's too late for me.
PETER: It's never too late, Vivian.
(Vivian looks out window)
VIVIAN: There, see?
PETER: What?
VIVIAN: In the back, out there. That's our dogwood.
(Peter looks out)
PETER: A dogwood is a tree though...isn't it, Vivian?
VIVIAN: Yup.
PETER: Well, that's a tree stump, Vivian. I don't see a...that's a tree stump.
VIVIAN: Well, just under that tree, Scott and Stanley buried Scott's goldfish. I forget what his name was.
PETER: Ya can't live in the past, Vivian.
VIVIAN: Champion! Champion the goldfish. Champion was his full name, but Scott used to call him Champ, for short.
PETER: You do this every night?
VIVIAN: Oh, I know it's silly. But I like it. I like comin' down here and putzin' around.
PETER: Well, yeah, that's all fine and good, Vivian, but it seems to me that everything you say you have...doesn't exist.
VIVIAN: What do ya mean?

PETER: I mean I couldn't see anything you just pointed out to me right now with my eyes. And come to think of it, that goes for Kelly too, and this whole thing with Scott --

VIVIAN: -- well, maybe I just figure, that sometimes, Peter, it's better to settle for the next best thing.

PETER: Which is what?

VIVIAN: Well, not what I have right now, but what I make out of what I used to have.

PETER: Well, Vivian, I think you really oughta reassess your priorities. And let me tell ya somethin' else; after tomorrow, when I start makin' the big bucks, you and Stan are goin' to China, on me! We're gonna expand your world if it takes a mental crowbar to do it. And we'll get you outa this little kitchen...and we'll get you a new tree...and a new set of glasses...and a new dog...that's alive...with a real bark. No more of this recorded dog stuff.

VIVIAN: Oh, you're a good boy, Peter. But I don't know. I like my little kitchen the way it is. (Vivian moves toward the door) Don't stay up too late. And turn out the lights when you're done.

PETER: I will.

(Vivian suddenly moves toward Peter, kisses him on the cheek)

VIVIAN: Goodnight, honey.

PETER: (Surprised) Yeah, Vivian, goodnight. (Just as Vivian is about to leave the kitchen, Peter turns to her) China, Vivian, on me. (Vivian turns to Peter, smiles, then exits. Peter is frozen for a moment, then goes to his briefcase and takes out a few of his books. He sets himself to practice his presentation. He laughs a little, lightly, then...) The great industrialist Henry Ford once remarked, "A man's ability to communicate his..." (Peter is suddenly distracted, looks toward the glass) "Effective speech is the bridge on which..." (Peter is again distracted. He slowly goes over to the glass, and after looking at it a moment, warily, goes and picks it up. He holds it in his hand, gazing at it until the lights fade slowly to black)

Act Two, Scene Three

(As the lights come up, we see Vivian in an apron, standing
near the entrance to the living room, holding a basket of
laundry. She is facing Stan as he opens the refrigerator
door)

VIVIAN: Stanley, what do ya want?

STANLEY: I'm gonna pour myself a soda. What is there a law
against that?

(A panicked look comes over Vivian's face)

VIVIAN: Why don't you just let me get it for you, Stanley. I'll be
right there.

(Stan removes the bottle of 7-Up from the fridge, closes the
door)

STAN: I can do it myself! Just don't be hoverin' around me like
you're always doin'. (Vivian quickly turns, runs into the living
room, puts the laundry basket down. Stan walks toward the
table with the bottle, twisting the cap. Vivian runs back into the
kitchen, runs to the stove, grabs an empty pot and moves
cautiously toward Stan) What are you doin'?

(Vivian freezes)

VIVIAN: Nothin', Stanley. Just watchin'.

(Stan walks toward the table, tipping the bottle well left of the
intended glass. Vivian, pot in hand, begins to sneak closer to
him, trying to place the pot directly under the bottle, pre-
venting a major flood. Just as she is about to reach him,
Stan turns toward her again)

STAN: Are you hoverin' again?

(Vivian quickly tip toes back toward the stove, trying to
"throw" her voice as it were, miming as though she were
wiping the counter)

VIVIAN: No, Stanley! No! I'm just wipin', that's all. Just
wipin'.

STAN: Alright, then.

(Stan turns the bottle back toward the glass, tilts it, and proceeds to pour the soda all over the chair next to the table. Vivian looks on, wincing as Peter walks through the door, his head hung low)

VIVIAN: Peter!

PETER: Hey.

STAN: What's up, kid?

PETER: Hey, Stan.

VIVIAN: Peter, what's the matter? What happened?

PETER: Oh, nothin' Vivian, you know, same pathetic friggin' thing that happens every day of my life. Miss my bus, finally get the local, wait an hour in traffic just to get through the tunnel, finally get in, step in a huge puddle, hail a cab, get to the hotel, nail my presentation, get another cab back, get ripped off by the driver who that's right, doesn't have change for a twenty...

VIVIAN: Peter...

PETER: Yeah, Vivian?

VIVIAN: You got it? You got the job?

PETER: Yeah, Vivian, didn't I mention that already?

(Peter finally cracks a smile)

VIVIAN: Peter!

STAN: Hey!

VIVIAN: Peter, that's wonderful.

PETER: Cripes, Vivian, you seem all surprised. I mean was there ever any doubt?

(Peter winks at Vivian)

STAN: When do ya start?

PETER: They're gonna call me to firm up the starting dates. And are ya listening to me, Stan...my "monetary" compensation as well.

VIVIAN: Oh, Peter.

STAN: Not, bad. Not bad.

PETER: Vivian, when that phone rings you have to be Mrs. Merkel again.

VIVIAN: But I am Mrs. Merkel.

PETER: No, my secretary Mrs. Merkel.

VIVIAN: Oh. Yeah.

STAN: Hey, now what is that?

VIVIAN: So what did ya do, Peter? Did ya talk?

PETER: Did I talk? I didn't shut up! (Peter pulls a chair out from the table, sitting on it backwards. Suddenly he notices the puddle on it) What the...

VIVIAN: Go on, honey. Tell us what happened.

PETER: (Standing) Okay, I get in there and granted, okay, I see they're a little "so so" about me at first. I think it was my scar to tell ya the truth...I mean, you know my bowling scar...and this one assistant manager guy kinda keeps lookin' at it, but I just wink at 'im ya know, every time his eyes drift over to it, I just wink at him and laugh a little, lightly, you know just like I said, but all the time I was floatin', ya know? Floatin' on a cloud of gilded verbosity...and watchin' 'em, each one of 'em, one by one, comin' over to me, comin' over to my side, my way of seein' things until just a few seconds away from where I felt like I might actually be losin' 'em... I'm saved.

STAN/ VIVIAN: How?

PETER: By a little mouse in the corner... some business manager accountant type pip squeak, just the type a' guy that'll swing a vote, either way, sittin' over there in the corner, eatin' his little corn muffin, rippin' into it like a rat to cheese, ignorin' me until suddenly I stop... and I look at him... and he looks at me... (Snaps his fingers) and I clinch it, right there.

STAN: What do ya mean?

VIVIAN: What did ya say?

PETER : I said "excuse me, I don't mean to take us all out of this little rhythm we got goin' here, but aren't those socks that you have on what are commonly referred to as "argyle" socks?" He stops chewin', everybody's breathless. He looks down at his socks, up at me, shakes his head. I pause, shake my head a little and lob it back; "Sorry, it's just that I thought that *that* kind of style, that kind of quiet understated attention to detail had been lost to us forever. At least as far as fashion goes that is."

VIVIAN: Wow.

PETER: So I go on with my spiel and out the side of my eye I can see this dweeb's face positively beaming, color coming back to his face for the first time in friggin' years as he sits straight up...and I conclude my presentation, real quiet like, smile, shake a few hands...a hushed whispered conversation with the manager, a gentlemen's agreement that I'll be back, that we're gonna be able to work together and I float outa there, not a whisper, not a sound...just a trail of my having been there, lingering like that ...but silent...(Pause)

VIVIAN: Isn't that somethin', Stanley?

PETER: (Earnest, to Vivian) You have to be a good Mrs. Merkel this time, Vivian. Only this time I'm home, I mean, I'm in my office.

STAN: Hey, c'mon, this ain't your office.

VIVIAN: I'll do it good, Peter. Let me just go upstairs and get you a towel.

PETER: Great!

(Vivian goes into the house. Stan stands there silently, turning a little away from Peter)

PETER: I didn't disappoint ya, did I, Stan?

STAN: What do ya mean?

PETER: I mean you know, by not disappointing ya?

(Beat. The phone rings)

PETER: Holy shit!

STAN: What!?

PETER: Vivian!? (Peter runs into the house, screams up the stairs) Vivian, get down here! You have to be Mrs. Merkel!

(Ring. We hear Vivian from upstairs)

VIVIAN: (Off) What did you say, honey?

PETER: I SAID, YOU HAVE TO GET DOWN HERE, NOW!

VIVIAN: (Off) I can't hear ya, honey. I'll be down in a minute.

PETER: Oh, my God! (Ring. Peter runs back into the kitchen) Stan!

(Ring)

STAN: What?

PETER: *You* are Mrs. Merkel!

STAN: What?

(Ring)

PETER: Just fake it...fake it! (Peter picks up the phone,
thrusting it into Stan's hand, whispering...) Say something...
say something...
(Stan, disoriented, puts the phone to his ear, clears his throat,
gruffly announcing...)

STAN: Uh...I'm...uh...I'm Mrs. Merkel.
(Peter grabs the phone out of Stan's hand, partially covering
the receiver with his own)

PETER: Uh...thank you so much retarded Uncle Edgar...thank
you for visiting me here at my office, but I better get back to
work now.

STAN: What are ya...?
(Peter lifts the phone to his ear, Vivian finally enters, holding
a towel)

PETER: Hogancamp...ah, yes, Mr. Kinghorn, of course.

VIVIAN: Oh, boy...
(Peter shushs Vivian)

PETER: ...why sure, sure... well I... I certainly felt that way too.
In fact I was just telling Mrs. Merkel... (Vivian smiles, proud)
...right ... well now that's a good point, Mr. Kinghorn, and one
that I think we shouldn't shy away from exploring, because...
uh huh... right... well if anyone would have the breadth of
knowledge to make that sort of... right... well how couldn't I?
(Peter fakes a long laugh) And for my part I couldn't be more
appreciative of your... oh, right, please, you're a busy man. I'm
very much looking forward to that opportunity ... yes, Sir, and
I... right... sure I will... I am quite confident of that. (Fake
laugh) One thing I am curious about Mr... okay, sure thing...
alrighty, then... talk to ya soon. (Peter hangs up) Well, okay,
that's not... no... that's not bad.

VIVIAN: What did he say?

STAN: Did he try to talk ya down?

PETER: No, actually I didn't get it. Uhm. (Pause) I uh... well, he... what happened was...it's interesting, because uhm...are you guys hungry, yet? I'm starvin'. Actually in the end it must've been that guy with the uh...I meant to buy my own soda, Vivian, I don't mean to keep drinkin' your...I guess if I had to break it down...am I the only one hungry, here, because if you guys wanna wait...see my head just...see that's the...
(Peter stands there, frozen)
VIVIAN: Peter, honey, are you alright?
PETER: I'm fine, Vivian, really. Let's not...you know, let's not...I just think the important thing to remember is...
STAN: --you're better off. You're better off not gettin' what ya wanted.
(Peter turns toward Stan. Glares at him. Vivian is suddenly uneasy)
PETER: What?
VIVIAN: Peter, honey, take Kelly for a walk.
PETER: No, wait. What did you just say, Stanley? What did you just say to me?
VIVIAN: Peter...
STAN: Now you know who you are, see? See times like this is when you get down to it. When you begin to see who you are. Now you know what you're talkin' about. NOW you can talk in public.
(Pause. Peter jerks the bat out of Stan's hand. Stan falters)
VIVIAN: Peter...what are you doing?
(Peter handles the bat wildly)
STAN: What are you doin'? Give me that.
PETER: You are a fascinating man, Stanley Merkel, you really are.
VIVIAN: Peter, honey, please...
STAN: Look, I ain't makin' any kinda fun of ya, I'm just sayin', that's all. Now you know who you are. Nobody's anybody, til they know who they are!
PETER: So what are you, Stanley, huh? What are you?
STAN: All I'm tellin' ya is what I told Scott before ya--

PETER: --look, I don't want to hear anymore shit about Scott! If he's such a great guy, why isn't he still here listening to all your history bullshit like I am!

VIVIAN: Peter--

PETER: --and why doesn't he call Stan, huh!?

VIVIAN: Peter--

PETER: --why doesn't he call!?

(Vivian goes to the recorder, pressing it down. We hear Kelly's "barking" continuously)

VIVIAN: Peter, take Kelly for a walk.

(Peter swings the bat wildly)

PETER: I bet you gave him the same history lesson you gave me, right Stan?

(Barking)

VIVIAN: Peter, please --

PETER: -- well I don't blame him for not comin' back! (Reacting to bark) Vivian, Christ!

STAN: Hey! You don't know Scott! You don't know nothin'! See he never knew who he was! You're gettin' to know who you are, see, and that's good!

PETER: Vivian, Christ! WILL YOU SHUT THAT FUCKIN' THING UP!

(Peter suddenly lunges for the recorder, grabbing the tape out of it and smashing the cassette violently on the counter. Stan calls out, horrified for Vivian)

STAN: Vivian!?

VIVIAN: I'm alright, Stanley. I'm alright.

(Peter looks at what he's done)

PETER: Jesus...

(Stan suddenly turns toward Peter, violently taking him by his collar and pushing him against the counter)

STAN: Don't you EVER talk to your mother like that, do you understand me?!

PETER: (Struggling to breathe) Hey...

VIVIAN: Stanley, no!

STAN: And don't you EVER show your face in this house again--
VIVIAN: --Stanley!
STAN: --YOU ARE NO SON OF MINE, DO YOU HEAR
 WHAT I'M SAYIN' TO YOU!! (Peter pushes Stan off)
PETER: Get off me! Who the hell do ya think you're talkin' to
 here! What the...? (Stan steps back, disoriented. Peter looks at
 both Vivian and Stan) Jesus...
 (Vivian moves to Stan)
VIVIAN: It's alright, Stanley. It's alright.
 (Peter quickly runs upstairs. Vivian looks to Stan)
VIVIAN: Be careful what you say to him, Stanley, he's still only
 a boy.
STAN: He's right, though.
VIVIAN: About what?
STAN: Scott ain't never gonna call again. He ain't never gonna
 call again.
 (Peter enters the kitchen, suitcase in hand)
VIVIAN: Peter, what are you doing?
PETER: I gotta go, Vivian. I gotta... I'm sorry about...
VIVIAN: ...Peter, you don't have to go.
PETER: No, I gotta lot to do, Vivian. Do I owe ya any money?
VIVIAN: No, honey. Now c'mon, I'll make some supper.
PETER: I can't Vivian, really. It's no big deal. (Peter moves to
 the door, picking up his briefcase off the table. As he moves
 toward the door with it, he suddenly stops, shaking the
 briefcase. He looks toward Stan) Oh, yeah, Stan. I almost
 forgot. (Peter moves over to Stan. He takes Stan's hand and
 puts it around the handle of the briefcase) These are for you.
STAN: What?
PETER: Inside...there's a couple of rocks I got for ya. And
 they're real, don't worry about it. I dug down like two feet to
 get 'em. They're real, Stan. You were right all along.
 (Peter heads toward the door)

VIVIAN: Peter, your briefcase.
(Peter stops, turns to Vivian)
PETER: I'm not gonna need it anymore, Vivian. You keep it.
VIVIAN: But --
PETER: -- you keep it. (Pause) I'll see ya.
(Peter quickly kisses Vivian, then heads out. The door slams hard. Vivian stands frozen, looking toward the door. After a moment, Stan slowly makes his way over to the phone, picks it up. Vivian turns to him)
VIVIAN: Stanley, what are you doing?
STAN: I'm gonna call my kid. What is there a law against that?

(Vivian's face begins to glow with a smile as she turns, looks in the wake of Peter and then back to Stan as music comes up and the lights slowly fade to black)

THE END

TRACES

To Kathleen

"Traces" was first produced in a workshop at The Yale School of Drama with the following cast:

Helen: Roxanna Augesen
Norman: Sean Haberle
Mrs. Krazner: Julie Lawrence
Pauly: Enrico Colantoni

The director was Mark Rucker.

The Characters

HELEN: Late twenties, early thirties. Blind

NORMAN: Twenties to forties

MRS. KRAZNER: Sixties

PAULY: Twenties to fifties

The Setting and Time

The play takes place in Helen's living room, in a small apartment behind the boardwalk in Atlantic City, New Jersey. Helen's apartment is half of a two family house she shares with Mrs. Krazner, next door.

Everything in the apartment seems antiquated, and gives the impression of being objects in a museum, untouched for years.

There's a couch, with an old broken clock on the mantle, a couple of chairs, a table with several envelopes on it, a set of encyclopedias on a shelf in the back, two doors; one leading to the kitchen, as well as one leading to the outside, a staircase in back, that leads upstairs, and a small dust covered mirror hanging on the back wall.

The time is the present.

(As the lights come up, we see the apartment empty for a moment. Then, the kitchen door creeks open, and a strange light cuts across the room. Helen enters, calling out behind her)

HELEN: Please, come in. I'm sorry if it's very dark in here. I don't get much sunlight anymore since they built up all these buildings around me.

MAN: (Off) Oh, yeah, yeah, no problem.

(The man enters behind Helen, dressed like a street person. He stands in the darkness)

HELEN: Thank you so much for helping me. You're very kind.

MAN: Hey, no problem.

HELEN: Here, I'll get a light. (Helen turns on a light. We see she's carrying an umbrella she apparently uses as a cane. She also has a ripped bag of groceries in her hand. The man is standing still, carrying a few of the grocery items. He has a bad cut, and appears to be bleeding on his forehead) I don't know why they started using these silly plastic bags. They have to be triple bagged, just to make them as strong as one paper bag...plus, as far as I know, they're not biodegradable.

MAN: Yeah, yeah I know. I hate that. I really hate them that they're not that. I hate that.

HELEN: Well...thank you for helping me. Mrs. Krazner, next door, usually does my shopping for me. It's not that I can't go out...it's just...well I can't chase a can of soup down the street...

MAN: Oh no, no. Yeah...I mean that's most...you know...right of you. I mean I'm surprised they don't think of that. Double bagging I mean...you know...for blind people most especially. Because...you know...I mean, they are blind and stuff.

HELEN: Yes, well...thank you. (The man pauses for a moment, looking at the door cautiously. Suddenly he fakes a sneeze, but rather poorly)

HELEN: Oh...was...was that a sneeze?

MAN: Uh...yeah. Yeah, it was.

HELEN: Do you have a cold?

MAN: Yeah I do. Do you happen to have a tissue Ma'am...and perhaps a band aid of some kind?

HELEN: Why, do you have a cut?

MAN: More like a blister, really.

HELEN: Oh. Well...alright. I'll be right back.

MAN: Thank you. Thank you, Madam...very much.

(Helen goes into the kitchen. As soon as she does, the man runs to the door, quickly looks outside it, then quietly closes it. He then looks out the window. Helen comes in again with a band aid and a tissue)

HELEN: Here you are.

(She hands him the tissue and band aid)

MAN: Oh thank you Ma'am...very much.

HELEN: (Extending her hand) My name is Helen.

MAN: (Shaking) Oh yeah? Well, that's great.

(Pause)

HELEN: And yours?

MAN: Oh uhm...well, uh...Norman actually. Well, no! I mean my first name is uh...

HELEN: ...Norman.

MAN: No.

HELEN: Oh, "Mr. Norman."

MAN: No...well yeah. Well, both really.

HELEN: What?

MAN: Both. My first name and my last name are both the same...Norman.

HELEN: Oh. Norman...Norman.

NORMAN: That's right. It's stupid, I know. My father named me, and he was uh...well, he was stupid.

HELEN: Oh. Well. I'm sorry.

NORMAN: That's okay. It's not your fault. (As Norman wipes the blood off his head we hear a helicopter approaching from the distance. The sound of it becomes quite loud as it passes over head, eventually fading) Trump.

HELEN: What?
NORMAN: That's Trump.
HELEN: Who is that?
NORMAN: You don't know who Donald Trump is?
HELEN: No.
NORMAN: He flies all his high rollers down here in his
  helicopter.
HELEN: Oh, you mean the whirlybird?
NORMAN: What?
HELEN (Pointing up) The whirlybird.
NORMAN: Oh. Well...okay, sure. I guess, you know, whatever
  ya wanna call it. (Norman suddenly turns around, spooked)
NORMAN: What was that?
HELEN: What?
NORMAN: That was weird.
HELEN: What, Mr. Norman?
NORMAN: You didn't feel that?
HELEN: What?
NORMAN: I coulda sworn somebody was right here, standin'
  next to me...only I couldn't see anybody and...
HELEN: --it was cold.
NORMAN: How did you know that?
HELEN: Intuition.
NORMAN: (After a pause) Yeah, well...I better get back to the
  uh...I'm in a convention here, of uh...doctors. You know,
  we're all here to meet in a convention and stuff.
HELEN: Oh, you're a doctor?
NORMAN: That's right.
HELEN: My father was a doctor.
NORMAN: Oh...great.
HELEN: He worked out of St. Anne's. I never saw him there,
  though. He died before I was born.
NORMAN: Oh, sorry Helen.
HELEN: What do you specialize in, Dr. Norman?
NORMAN: Oh uhm...you know...(Looking down in a panic)
  Feet. Feet...and uh...ankles and stuff.

HELEN: Podiatry.

NORMAN: That's right.

HELEN: It's a podiatry convention.

NORMAN: I guess you could call it that, yeah. (Pause) I'm fine, thanks.

HELEN: I'm sorry?

NORMAN: Oh, I'm sorry. I thought you just asked me if I wanted something to drink.

HELEN: Well...no. I don't think I said anything, did I?

NORMAN: Well, I couldn't anyway, Helen...I really oughta be uh...(Norman fakes a sneeze again. This time a little better) Damn cold.

HELEN: Would you like an aspirin or something?

NORMAN: Would it be putting you out?

(Helen moves toward the kitchen, then stops)

HELEN: Actually, I was going to have some tea, Dr. Norman. Would you like some too? I could put some honey in it, for your throat.

NORMAN: I guess one cup wouldn't hurt, Helen. Thanks.

(Helen goes into the kitchen. Norman dashes to the window and looks out, pulling the shade down. Helen enters)

HELEN: It won't take long.

NORMAN: Great.

HELEN: Please, sit down.

(They sit)

NORMAN: Boy, your furniture is really well... preserved.

HELEN: It's all my mother's. I didn't see the point of buying anything new since I couldn't see it anyway...and this furniture is the last thing I remember seeing, really.

NORMAN: "Remember," seeing?

HELEN: I only started not being able to see when I was nineteen, Dr. Norman. The couch you're sitting on is green...

NORMAN: Right...

HELEN: And directly behind you are my father's old encyclopedias. I suppose by now they're pretty outdated.

NORMAN: Yeah, I guess so.

HELEN: And right over there is my mother's old clock. It has her
initials on it, to the left of the two. Can you see them?
(Norman gets up, inspects clock)
NORMAN: Oh yeah. It isn't workin', though. I could toy around
with it for ya. I'm pretty good at this kinda stuff.
(Helen quickly takes the clock back from Norman, puts it back
on the mantle)
HELEN: I like it just how it is, thank you, Dr. Norman. Would
you like something in your tea?
NORMAN: No, plain is good Helen, thanks.
(Helen goes into the kitchen again. Norman runs to the window,
looks out, pensive. Helen comes through the kitchen door
with two cups of tea, handing one to Norman)
HELEN: Here you are.
NORMAN: Oh, thanks.
(They sit)
HELEN: So, Dr. Norman. Why did you and all the other
podiatrists decide to come to Atlantic City?
NORMAN: Well...I mean, you know...when ya think about it,
there's as many feet here as there are anywhere else I guess.
And you know, plus there's the boardwalk... which every-
body ...you know, "walks on." And that's with their feet.
So. That's gonna add up to a lot of people walkin' on their
feet... and that's even times two really, since you know,
everybody has two feet. So I guess we all figured we might as
well come here.
HELEN: Oh. Well...
NORMAN: --what about you, Helen, do you work?
HELEN: Yes, I have one of those "work at home" jobs. Mostly
I just stuff envelopes, since it's one of the few things a blind
person could do that isn't really a "blind person's job."
NORMAN: But aren't you scared you're gonna get stuff turned
around upside down in the envelope?
HELEN: Oh no, Dr. Norman, let me show you. (Helen goes to
the table with the envelopes and proceeds to do everything she
describes. Norman ignores her, peaking out the window)

HELEN: (Cont) See I get everything set up the way it should be, envelopes on the left, filling material on the right. Then I just sit down in front of the table...grab the filling material with my right hand... what are you standing by the window for Dr. Norman, are you looking for something?

NORMAN: No, no Helen, I was just seein' what the weather was like out. That's all.

HELEN: You seem a little nervous, is everything alright?

NORMAN: Oh yeah.

HELEN: I'm sorry if I'm boring you.

NORMAN: No, no...you're not boring me. It's kinda like a little system you got worked out, huh?

HELEN: Well when you're blind, you have to live by systems.

NORMAN: Yeah well, when you can see ya have to live by 'em too.

(The doorbell rings. Norman instinctively moves away from the door and pulls out a gun from his jacket. He stands frozen, pointing it toward the door)

HELEN: What's the matter, Dr. Norman?

NORMAN: (Shaking) It's your doorbell, Helen.

HELEN: I know, but is there something wrong?

NORMAN: Well no, not necessarily. Why, who do ya think it is?

HELEN: I don't know. I'll answer it.

(Helen goes toward the door)

NORMAN: No, wait Helen! You really shouldn't stand right in front of the door like that.

HELEN: Why not?

(Doorbell rings again)

NORMAN: I just think it would be better...if, when you ask who it is, that you stand on the side of the door, behind the wall...and then ask. I know it's none of my business, but I'm just sayin', that's all.

HELEN: Alright. (Helen goes to the side of the door by the wall, yells out...) Who is it?

VOICE: Helen it's me, open the door.

HELEN: (Whispering) Oh no, it's Mrs. Krazner.

NORMAN: Can I use your bathroom, Helen?

HELEN: Oh yes, please Dr. Norman, go ahead. Upstairs to the right. And take all the time you need.

NORMAN: Oh, I will.

MRS. KRAZNER: (Knocking) Helen, what's goin' on in there?

(Norman sprints up the stairs as Helen opens the front door)

HELEN: I'm sorry, Mrs. Krazner.

(Mrs. Krazner enters wearing a senior citizens bowling league jacket and carrying a cup of sugar)

MRS. KRAZNER: What the heck is going on here?

HELEN: Nothing, I was just making sure it was you.

MRS. KRAZNER: Since when do ya have to make sure it's me?

HELEN: I was just being safe.

MRS. KRAZNER: Huh. Well... here's the sugar I borrowed.

(She hands Helen the sugar)

HELEN: Thank you.

(Mrs. Krazner inspects the living room)

MRS. KRAZNER: I just wanted to make sure you got home alright.

HELEN: Oh, I'm fine. I just had a little accident, that's all.

MRS. KRAZNER: What accident?

HELEN: Oh, nothing bad. The bag I was using broke, and if it weren't for Dr. Norman...

MRS. KRAZNER: --who's Dr. Norman?

HELEN: He's the man who helped me bring the rest of my groceries home. I got everything back except for my Pillsbury cinnamon rolls, because Dr. Norman said they rolled right down the sewer.

MRS. KRAZNER: Oh, that's a shame. Where is Dr. Norman now?

HELEN: He's gone, Mrs. Krazner. He left.

MRS. KRAZNER: Really?

HELEN: Yes. (Pause) Well, I suppose you'll want to get back home yourself.

MRS. KRAZNER: I "suppose" so. (Helen leads Mrs. Krazner toward the door) If there's anything you need dear...

HELEN: --thank you, I'm fine.

MRS. KRAZNER: Are you sure you don't want me to make a sandwich for ya?

HELEN: I'm sure. Thank you very much.

(Helen closes the door behind Mrs. Krazner. Just as she does, we see Norman coming down the stairs)

NORMAN: God, what a nightmare she is.

HELEN: She means well, Dr. Norman.

(Pause)

NORMAN: Why didn't you tell her I was here?

HELEN: Oh I couldn't. I mean with you being a man and all, I wouldn't want her to think that I was...you know...that I was...well...

NORMAN: Yeah. Well, you really oughta tell her to butt out next time. I mean who does she think she is, snoopin' around like that?

HELEN: I suppose I just got used to it. I do get tired of getting all these cups of sugar though. She keeps returning all these cups of sugar, and I don't remember ever lending them out to her.

NORMAN: Well see that's what I'm talking about, Helen. That's why she's a nightmare.

HELEN: I could show you in my pantry, Dr. Norman. I have at least seventy-two pounds of sugar...in plastic bags...all stacked up, one on top of the other!

NORMAN: Well, Helen...

HELEN: --but she does mean well.

NORMAN: ...sure. (Pause)

HELEN: Well...

NORMAN: Yeah, well I guess I uh...

HELEN: --where are you and all the other podiatrists staying?

NORMAN: Oh, the uh...the Eldorado, over on Iowa.

HELEN: Is it nice?

NORMAN: Yeah, it's near the casinos and stuff.

HELEN: Have you been playing all the gambling games while you've been here?

NORMAN: Well, I'm not much of a gambler myself. What about you?

HELEN: No, I've never even been in one of those places. My mother was alive when they started building them... but... she was sick... and I just stayed in here for what seemed like years... taking care of her. Plus my eyes weren't getting any better, and I hardly had time to worry about what was going on around me...and by the time she passed away, I could hardly see at all. So as far as I know, Atlantic City is still just a small town by the ocean.

NORMAN: Yeah well, it isn't small anymore. Trust me.

HELEN: Mrs. Krazner says all the casinos look like big fancy wrapped up Christmas boxes, with electric lights on them.

NORMAN: Yeah well, I guess she's right.

HELEN: Ever since they built the place up though, I can't hear the ocean anymore. I used to be able to.

NORMAN: Even from here?

HELEN: Oh, yes. Late at night...if you listened real quiet...and you set your mind on nothing else but listening for them...you could hear the waves breaking hard...one after the other...and after awhile it would put you to sleep until it woke you up again the next morning. But now all I hear is people screaming ...and laughing...don't you? And ringing...always ringing.

NORMAN: Those are the slots over at Ballys.

HELEN: I tried ordering one of those tapes they play the sound of the ocean on. But they're no good, because the rhythm on the tape isn't natural. It's the same wave breaking over and over again, and recorded one thousand times. And instead of putting you to sleep, it gives you a migraine.

NORMAN: Well, that sucks.

HELEN: It's alright, though. I put ear plugs in my ears now...so I can't hear anything. Which I suppose is better than hearing something you don't want to.

NORMAN: I guess.

HELEN: Are you from New Jersey, Dr. Norman?

NORMAN: Yeah, Freehold. But I was born in Hoboken.

HELEN: Oh, you and Frank Sinatra.

NORMAN: That's right.

HELEN: Mrs. Krazner says he has his footprints over on the boardwalk now.

NORMAN: Yeah, in front of Resorts. I stand right inside 'em sometimes, for good luck.

HELEN: Oh so...you have been here before.

NORMAN: Yeah, didn't I say? A couple times.

HELEN: Are you married, Dr. Norman?

NORMAN: Excuse me, Helen?

HELEN: Oh, I'm sorry. I didn't mean...I mean I'm not...I didn't mean...I mean I didn't...

NORMAN: Oh no, that's okay, Helen. No. No, I'm not. How 'bout you?

HELEN: Me?

NORMAN: Yeah.

HELEN: Oh no, I'm not. I mean I never even...why, do you think I seem like I could be?

NORMAN: Yeah, why not?

HELEN: I don't know. Thank you. I mean for even thinking I could be.

NORMAN: Sure, no problem, Helen.

(Norman suddenly sees something pass by the window, near the door. He reaches for his gun. The doorbell rings. He points the gun straight toward the door)

HELEN: Oh no, it's probably Mrs. Krazner again.

NORMAN: Yeah, but remember what we said last time Helen, you could never be sure.

HELEN: Oh I'm sure. She probably came by to borrow something she wants to return again later. Would you mind going to the bathroom again, Dr. Norman?

(Helen moves toward door)

NORMAN: Wait Helen, remember what I said.

HELEN: What?

NORMAN: Don't stand in front of the door.

HELEN: Oh, I'm sure it's okay. (The doorbell rings again. Helen yells through the door) Mrs. Krazner? (No answer) Mrs. Krazner? (Pause) That's funny, you'd think she'd say something.

NORMAN: (Under his breath) Shit.

HELEN: Oh you know, it's probably the Kaminski boys. They're always playing games like this.

(Helen starts to open door)

NORMAN: (Lunging toward her) No Helen, wait!

HELEN: (Opening door) It's alright. (As Helen opens the door, the daylight pours in. There appears to be no one there. Norman stands behind Helen, pointing his gun over her shoulder, shaking) Hello? Hello, is anyone there?

NORMAN: Nobody's there. Nobody's there, Helen.

HELEN: Well then it's probably the Kaminskis. (Helen steps in the doorway) Oh.

NORMAN: What?

HELEN: Nothing. I thought I heard someone running... but... no... (Helen closes the door. Norman puts his gun away, shaking) Are you alright, Dr. Norman?

NORMAN: Yeah Helen, why?

HELEN: Well you're breathing so heavily.

NORMAN: Oh well, you know Helen. It's really just stress. You know these foot conventions and stuff. It's stress, that's all. People don't appreciate all the stress people go through. You know, foot doctoring and stuff. It sounds like somethin' that might be real easy, just takin' care of people's feet, but it's not. You know, there's corns...and bunions and crap like that. Christ, everything. Do ya think I could have another cup of tea, Helen? I mean I don't want to intrude on your day or anything. I'm really just in no rush to get back to...you know, feet and stuff.

HELEN: Well sure Dr. Norman. I just assumed you had to get back.

NORMAN: Oh no, no. I'm okay with time I think, Helen. Plus I want to hear about... you know, I wanna hear more about the ocean and stuff, and Atlantic City bein' a small town, and stuff like that.

HELEN: Well okay, if you want, Dr. Norman. I'll be right back.

NORMAN: Thanks Helen. (Helen goes into the kitchen. Norman runs over to the window and peers out. He then goes to the phone on Helen's table. He reaches into his pocket, finds a crumpled piece of paper, puts it on the table and dials very quickly. At first there seems to be no answer. Then someone comes on, Norman whispers) Lenny? Thank God. Listen, you have to do two things, fast. First...(Pause) Lenny, are you listening to me here? Lenny? Stop breathing, what are you doin'? (Norman laughs, nervous) Lenny, say somethin' here, you're makin' me nervous. (Pause) Who is this? Who the hell is this? Who...? (Norman hangs up, fast. Helen comes out of the kitchen, startling Norman) Helen! Oh Christ, yeah Helen. Thanks.

HELEN: What's the matter, Dr. Norman?

NORMAN: What do ya mean?

HELEN: You're breathing so heavily, I could hear it from here.

NORMAN: Oh it's just... you know...feet. I can't take it anymore Helen. I hate my job. I hate feet. I can't even look at my own feet when I'm takin' a shower, I hate 'em so much. I hate 'em. I hate 'em. (Helen hands him a cup of tea on a saucer)

HELEN: You're shaking.

NORMAN: No, I'm not.

HELEN: Your cup.

NORMAN: What about it?

HELEN: It's rattling in its saucer.

NORMAN: No it's not.

HELEN: Yes it is.

(Norman lifts his cup off the saucer)

NORMAN: No it's not Helen, see?

(Norman drifts toward the window)

HELEN: Why are you looking out the window again?

NORMAN: Do you ever think about death, Helen?

HELEN: What?

NORMAN: Death. You know, "not living." Do ya ever think about that?

HELEN: All the time.

NORMAN: Really?

HELEN: Yes.

NORMAN: Why?

HELEN: I don't know. I don't really have much else to do. I can't watch television, and the radio my mother bought me is broken.

NORMAN: Aren't you scared of it?

HELEN: No, not death. Dying I'm a little scared of sometimes, but not death.

NORMAN: What's the difference?

HELEN: Well, one I suppose I've seen before, but the other one I haven't.

NORMAN: Which one have ya seen?

HELEN: Dying.

NORMAN: Who...

HELEN: --my mother.

NORMAN: Oh yeah. Yeah, both my parents croaked too.

HELEN: So you think about death a lot too?

NORMAN: Well, just lately, to tell ya the truth. I've become sort of...pre-occupied with it. Which do ya think is worse; death, or dying?

HELEN: I really couldn't say. But from what I've seen, if death is worse than dying, than there's nothing worse than death.

NORMAN: What about living?

HELEN: Well, from what I could see, living is really the same thing as dying...because while you're taking care of one, the other one is being taken care of for you at the same time.

NORMAN: Well isn't that kind of a bummer of a way to look at things, Helen?

HELEN: What I'm saying isn't the way I'm choosing to look at things, it's just the way I see them.

NORMAN: Yeah well, I have to admit to ya right now, I'm
  scared of the whole shebang. I'm scared of living, because I
  know at some point, no matter when it is, I'm gonna die.
  And I know no matter how soon it is, I'm always gonna feel like
  it's too soon. And I'm scared of dyin', because I have a feeling
  that no matter how ya die, it's gonna hurt somehow. And I'm
  scared of death because I don't know after I die, whether or not
  I'll ever get the chance to live again. But that's stupid anyway,
  isn't it, Helen? Because I just said I was scared of living in the
  first place... and so what the hell am I complaining about? It's
  all just a vicious cycle anyway, isn't it?
HELEN: Well, I suppose it is...the way you describe it. But I'm
  sure there are other ways to look at something like that.
NORMAN: Something that "is," just "is" Helen.
HELEN: Not if you believe otherwise. I think there's always a
  way around vicious cycles, Dr. Norman. I think there's always
  a way to cheat them.
NORMAN: Cheat them?
HELEN: Yes, like living and dying. See the reason I'm not scared
  of them anymore, is because if you look at the both of them like
  they're any old game you've ever played on a playground when
  you were a child, then you could make up your own, new rules
  to play by, to suit yourself.
NORMAN: New rules?
HELEN: You must've played some kind of game when you were
  a child, Dr. Norman. Wasn't it always true, that if ever you
  were on a team that was losing... and there was no way you
  could ever catch up... the first thing you or someone else on
  your team would do, is raise your hand and yell; "new rule!"
  ...and make up some ridiculous rule that would make it almost
  impossible for the other team... in whatever you were
  playing... to ever score a point again?
NORMAN: Yeah, but that was cheating.
HELEN: To the winning team it was cheating, but to the losing
  team, it was just a new rule.
NORMAN: So?

HELEN: So, that's all I'm saying you have to do. Just raise your hand and yell "new rule!" I did.

NORMAN: How did you did?

HELEN: Well. I...

(Helen freezes)

NORMAN: What?

HELEN: It's just so strange.

NORMAN: What is?

HELEN: Talking to someone. I don't go out very much, Dr. Norman. Actually, before today... I just don't talk to people very much, and I suppose my head got dizzy, that's all... with the possibility of talking... I mean really talking to someone... back and forth. Face to face... like we're doing now.

NORMAN: Yeah, well...

HELEN: --you see there's a part of me that wants to just talk and talk and talk. To tell you or anyone, everything, just because it's all piled up inside... and sometimes I feel like if I don't let it out, it's just going to wither away.

NORMAN: Well, ya can't let that happen, Helen.

HELEN: Mrs. Krazner says that the world outside of ourselves isn't as safe as the world we make for ourselves inside. And that the best thing to do is to keep everything to yourself...and not to trust anyone.

NORMAN: (Looking out window) Well, ya gotta trust somebody.

HELEN: See, that's what I think too, Dr. Norman... that the whole world is as trustworthy as you make it, and that you could sooner trust someone you don't know... as you could trust someone you've known all your life.

NORMAN: Well, that's right.

HELEN: Then it is true...I could trust someone...anyone...even if I don't know them?

NORMAN: Well, sure Helen. That's what the world is based on, isn't it? Trust. (Pause)

HELEN: And I could trust you...couldn't I, Dr. Norman?

NORMAN: Well sure Helen, why not?

(Norman is just walking around, casually checking out the apartment, hardly paying attention to Helen)

HELEN: And I could talk to you...even about what I was talking about before...about how someone could make up a "new rule" for themselves...if they didn't feel like the old way of doing things was good enough?

NORMAN: Oh yeah, yeah Helen. Talk to me about that. I think that's very interesting.

HELEN: Do you really?

NORMAN: Oh yeah, yeah. Very interesting.

HELEN: Well, it's very simple, Dr. Norman. After my mother got sick, it started dawning on me that life, or, the whole "shebang" as you call it, is really just a game that everyone is predisposed to lose in the end.

NORMAN: (Looking out window) Well sure, sure.

HELEN: It was for my mother anyway. And she was always on the sidelines...just watching it...never even really wanting to play. I felt sometimes like she was a number drawn out of some great big lottery...and she was thrown...innocent...right into the arms of something so horrible, that all the rest of us could do was stand on the side of the bed...and watch. (Helen stops, turns toward Norman, who has begun listening a little more now) I don't expect any of this to mean anything to you, Dr. Norman. I'm not so selfish as to think that I'm the only one on the face of the earth to ever lose someone.

NORMAN: Oh no, Helen, it's alright.

HELEN: What was harder to see then anything else was her own ignorance of her situation. What I felt like I was watching, was the "her" inside herself that didn't have any idea, how wasted her body had become... and who kept trying, over and over again, with her eyes... to lift herself out of the bed she was dying in. And once in awhile, when the nurse and I would have to move her, to change her sheets... I would see her scream out in pain... only silently, because by then what was killing her had already spread to her throat... and so she was even denied the basic human right of screaming... or raging...against

HELEN: (Cont) what she had to feel was an injustice. Because in some world, I don't think this one, but in some world, what happened to her would have to be looked upon as cheating...on the world's part. Don't you think, Dr. Norman? Almost as if the world... or fate...or whatever, didn't have the courage to pick on anyone its own size. So it went for the easy mark. My mother. And it won. Granted. But not before I had the chance to raise my hand and yell..."new rule!" And I did.

NORMAN: What do ya mean, ya did?

HELEN: I mean I changed the rules, Dr. Norman. (Pause) I promised myself that her pain... that my mother's pain would be the last thing that I would let the world make me see. And it was.

NORMAN: Well...whoa, wait a minute here, Helen...

HELEN: When my mother first got sick, my eyesight was already beginning to fade. I knew the extent of the damage, and that if I did something about it, there wouldn't be any problem with my seeing...whatsoever. But every time I set my mind to doing something about it, my mother's situation, or her needs... would make my own little situation...seem even more little. And so by the time she died, I could hardly see at all. And by that time I had made a promise to myself to keep it that way. I promised, that I would never let the world make me see it take anything away from me ever again. Not like that. And I won't.

NORMAN: Whoa. Wait a minute here, Helen. Wait a minute.

HELEN: Now do you see what I mean, Dr. Norman? As far as I was concerned, there were never any official rules in the first place. So I just made up my own.

NORMAN: Wait, wait. What are you tellin' me here? Are you tellin' me you don't have to not see?

HELEN: No, I'm telling you I don't have to see, Dr. Norman. That's what I'm telling you.

NORMAN: Yeah, but...either way, you volunteered for being blind.

HELEN: I suppose that's one way of looking at it.

NORMAN: Well...what...what...well...God, Helen, I mean,
   God! That's a bad thing to do...that's a bad thing to do, Helen!
HELEN: Why?
NORMAN: Because it has to be against the law or somethin'.
HELEN: It's not against the law.
NORMAN: Well then...I mean that's gotta be against somethin'!
   It's against some kinda... well Cripes, it's against everything.
   It's bad. It's bad, Helen!
HELEN: You're the first person I ever told, Dr. Norman. You're
   the first person in the whole world, that I ever told.
NORMAN: Well Cripes, Helen, why?!
HELEN: Because, you said I could trust you.
NORMAN: Well stop! Stop trusting me. You don't even know
   who the hell I am, Helen...stop trusting me...God!
HELEN: But you said...you said "go ahead." You told me to say
   whatever I wanted. You said I could trust you. And I'm glad I
   did. I'm glad I told someone. It's like having a three hundred
   pound boulder of a secret lying on your shoulders for nine
   years...
NORMAN: --nine years!
HELEN: Yes, nine years!
   (Norman is backing away from Helen now, stunned)
NORMAN: Well Helen, I got news for ya. Because of all the
   people you could've trusted, you trusted the wrong one. Now
   take it back.
HELEN: Take what back?
NORMAN: What you just said. Let's both take it back, in our
   heads, right now. Let's erase what just happened here.
HELEN: You can't erase what happened.
NORMAN: Oh yes, we can. New rule! Starting right now, I know
   nothing. Wait, let me just ask ya one more thing before we
   erase, Helen.
HELEN: What?
NORMAN: You can't see now.
HELEN: That's right.

NORMAN: And you won't ever be able to see.

HELEN: Well no, not practically.

NORMAN: What do ya mean?

HELEN: I mean, not if I don't do anything about it. I suppose I could have an operation, but that isn't practical.

NORMAN: Why not?

HELEN: Because I don't want to, and even if I did, I could never afford it.

NORMAN: Great, so not only do you do something...how many years ago?

HELEN: Nine.

NORMAN: Nine years ago, that I know for sure, somehow, no matter what you tell me, is some kinda sick, mortal sin... but now you continue to do this sick, bad thing...for what? What do you plan to do...do this bad, evil thing for the rest of your life?

HELEN: I don't think it's a bad and evil thing.

NORMAN: (To himself) God, of all the friggin' houses...

HELEN: What do you mean by that?

(Suddenly the door opens, Mrs. Krazner enters)

MRS. KRAZNER: Helen?

HELEN: Mrs. Krazner.

(Mrs. Krazner sees Norman, stops in her tracks)

MRS. KRAZNER: Oh. My. God.

HELEN: What's the matter?

MRS. KRAZNER (To Norman) What the hell are you doing here?

HELEN: I live here.

(Mrs. Krazner dashes to the table, picks up the receiver end of the phone, holds it up as a weapon)

NORMAN: What are *you* doing here? Who do you think you are, burstin' into somebody's house like this?

MRS. KRAZNER: Helen, what has he done to you?

HELEN: Nothing, Mrs. Krazner, this is Dr. Norman.

NORMAN: Do you have a problem with that?

MRS. KRAZNER: (Wielding phone) Don't move, Mister! I don't know what you're pullin' here, but so help me, if you try any funny business, I'll "Dr Norman" you right in the head!

HELEN: Mrs. Krazner, what are you doing?

NORMAN: She's threatening me with your phone, Helen.

MRS. KRAZNER: Helen, call the police!

HELEN: Why, what's going on?

NORMAN: How is she gonna call the police, Mrs. Krazner, if you're holdin' up the phone like that?

MRS. KRAZNER: Call them in the kitchen, Helen!

HELEN: What's going on here!

MRS. KRAZNER: I'm saving your life!

NORMAN: How is it gonna make any difference if she calls 'em in the kitchen, if the line out here is off the hook?

MRS. KRAZNER: Alright, cut the crap, Mister got an answer for everything!

(Mrs. Krazner quickly puts down the receiver and picks up an ashtray)

NORMAN: What, no sugar this time, Mrs. Krazner?

MRS. KRAZNER: (Brandishing ashtray) Just you freeze right there, Mister!

HELEN: Mrs. Krazner, this is Dr. Norman.

MRS. KRAZNER: This is no doctor.

HELEN: Of course, he's a doctor.

MRS. KRAZNER: He's a bum! He's a bum Helen, look at 'im!

NORMAN: Oh, that's nice.

HELEN: He's not a bum.

MRS. KRAZNER: (To Norman) Tell her you're a bum. Tell her!

NORMAN: I'm not a bum, Mrs. Krazner.

MRS. KRAZNER: Well than tell her what you are, whatever it is.

HELEN: He's a doctor, Mrs. Krazner. He's...

NORMAN: --I'm not a doctor, Helen.

(Pause)

HELEN: What?

NORMAN: I'm not a doctor.

MRS. KRAZNER: See, what did I tell ya? Call the police, Helen.

NORMAN: But I'm not a bum either, Mrs. Krazner. And I didn't come here to hurt Helen.

MRS. KRAZNER: Yeah well, tell it to the cops, Mister wise aleck.

(Helen moves away from Norman, wary)

HELEN: Who are you then? Oh my God, who are you?

MRS. KRAZNER: He's a bum, Helen. I've seen 'im on the boardwalk a thousand times. He wants a quarter here, he wants a quarter there... (Norman moves) You make one move, and I'll "quarter you" right in the head!

(Norman starts to back up toward the front door)

NORMAN: Okay, okay, Mrs. Krazner, I'm just gonna back outa here, okay? No harm done.

MRS. KRAZNER: That's right, Mister... nice and slow. Call the police, Helen.

HELEN: (To Norman) Why did you do this to me?

NORMAN: (Backing out) Look, Helen, nothin' personal, okay?

MRS. KRAZNER: Nice and easy, Mister!

NORMAN: Hey, Mrs. Krazner, just chill, alright?

MRS. KRAZNER: Keep movin', smart aleck...(Norman turns, reaches for the doorknob, freezes. He looks at the door, then quickly sneaks a peak out the window) What are you doin'?

NORMAN: Helen...

HELEN: What?

MRS. KRAZNER: Hey...

NORMAN: Mrs. Krazner, be quiet, will ya? Helen, I just need to use your back door, okay?

HELEN: You can't.

MRS. KRAZNER: Watch it, Mister!

NORMAN: That's all I'm askin'.

(Norman moves toward the kitchen. Mrs. Krazner follows him with her ashtray)

MRS. KRAZNER: Nice and easy Mister...nice and easy.

NORMAN: Okay Mrs. Krazner, whatever you say.

HELEN: (To Norman) Wait a minute, who are you?

MRS. KRAZNER: 'Atta boy... nice and easy.

NORMAN: Okay, Mrs. Krazner, you got me scared outa my
boots here.
(Norman starts pushing open the kitchen door)
HELEN: Wait! Wait a minute!
(Norman stops)
MRS. KRAZNER: For what, Helen? What are you doin'?
HELEN: Mrs. Krazner, go home and wait for ten minutes. If I
don't call you back within that time...then you can call the
police and have them check on me.
MRS. KRAZNER: What? What are you doin'?
NORMAN: What *are* you doin', Helen?
HELEN: Please, Mrs. Krazner...
MRS. KRAZNER: The guy's a bum, Helen!
NORMAN: I'm not a bum, Mrs. Krazner.
HELEN: (Terse) Mrs. Krazner, I told you. If I don't call within
ten minutes, then call the police. Now please...
MRS. KRAZNER: Helen...
HELEN: (Again, firm) Mrs. Krazner, now!
(Pause. Mrs. Krazner slowly lowers her ashtray and moves to-
ward the front door, backing up, keeping her eye on Norman.
She stops)
MRS. KRAZNER: What would your mother think about this,
Helen? That's all I wanna know. What would your mother think
about this?
NORMAN: Hey, come on.
(Mrs. Krazner backs out, slamming the door in front of her.
Norman and Helen stand in the living room, frozen for a
moment, awkward. Then...)
HELEN: How could you?
NORMAN: Helen look, I didn't mean to do anything to you,
okay?
HELEN: You lied, and you stood there, acting like you were
someone else, while I told you...while I told you...
NORMAN: --hey look, I didn't tell ya to go ahead and blurt all
that stuff out, did I? I told ya to go ahead and tell me stuff, but
that doesn't mean ya go blabberin' out all your most intimate

NORMAN: (Cont) secrets and crap. I'm not gonna stand here and
feel bad about that, Helen. You oughta apologize to *me*...you
oughta feel bad for *me*...layin' all that stuff on somebody,
unprepared like that. You can't just tell people your life like
that, Helen, even if ya do know 'em!

HELEN: Why not?

NORMAN: Because...because it's just not like the world to do
somethin' like that. It's not right. Don't ya think people have
their own problems? Don't ya think people have their own
secrets... without somebody playing some kinda weird
game... for what? Nine years! And then, like they're tellin'
somebody they stole a box of candy or somethin', they admit
somethin' like what you admitted to me.

HELEN: Well excuse me if I trusted someone. Excuse me, if I
took a guess, or I took a gamble, that people...even in general... might be nicer than what I heard they were like.

NORMAN: Well see that's your problem, Helen.

HELEN: What?

NORMAN: All this stuff you hear, and don't see.

HELEN: I can't see!

NORMAN: You don't *want* to see, Helen, lets get it straight. You
are just like the rest of the world, hidin' from whatever it
doesn't want to see.

HELEN: And you're just the reason we don't want to see it.
You're a liar, and a cheat and a...and a...

NORMAN: --go ahead and say it, Helen. "Bum." Everybody else
does.

HELEN: I wasn't...

NORMAN: --and what makes ya think I don't hate bein' what I
am...or what everybody thinks I am. And that I don't have my
reasons for bein' it.

HELEN: I bet you do. And I bet I know more than you think I do.

NORMAN: Oh, really?

HELEN: I don't *not* know everything you know. You could play
all the games you want on a blind person, it isn't that hard. But
some things you can't keep from people.

NORMAN: Oh yeah? Like what, Helen...you're so smart.

HELEN: Like you're in trouble. There's some kind of something wrong with you. Something besides the fact that you're a liar.

NORMAN: Oh yeah? Like what, Helen? You're such the little detective.

HELEN: Something. Something that makes you breathe heavy, and your heart beat faster...almost so that I could hear it whenever the doorbell rings. Something that makes your tea cup shake like a leaf inside its saucer.

NORMAN: Is that right?

HELEN: That's right. And you're not a thief, because by now you would've taken something, and you're not here to do any harm to me, because by now you would've done it. So you must be here only because you don't want to be somewhere else.

NORMAN: Where?

HELEN: Anywhere. Anywhere but outside, where you could be seen.

(Norman squirms a little)

NORMAN: Well, well, Helen. I guess stayin' shut up in this place all these years has given you plenty of time to build up a fer-tile imagination.

HELEN: I "guess" so.

NORMAN: And I guess when ya can't watch T.V., ya gotta do somethin'...and I guess that somethin' for you is sittin' around thinkin' about death, and makin' up wild storybook fantasies inside your head.

HELEN: I "guess" so.

NORMAN: Well.

HELEN: Well, I suppose you'll want to get going.

NORMAN: I "guess" so.

HELEN: Well please, let me get the door for you.

(Helen moves to the front door)

NORMAN: I'll go out the back, Helen.

HELEN: Oh no, I wouldn't have it. (Pause) Besides, I don't have a back door.

(Helen begins to open the front door. Norman jumps out of the
sight of the open door, crouching behind the rail of the stair-
case. As Helen opens the door, the daylight rushes in)
HELEN: Is there something wrong, "Dr. Norman?"
NORMAN: Alright, alright, Helen.
HELEN: Are you normally so afraid of people's front doors?
NORMAN: Alright Helen, close the door.
HELEN: Maybe I should go outside and make sure "the coast is
clear." Isn't that how they say it?
NORMAN: Close the door!
(Helen slams the door shut. Pause. Norman comes out from
behind the rail)
HELEN: You're breathing heavily again.
(The phone rings. Helen answers it)
HELEN: Hello?...Oh, Mrs. Krazner. No, no, everything is fine.
No, no I'm alright, but thank you very much...alright, that's
fine...bye bye. (She hangs up, turns to Norman) So tell me,
"Dr. Norman," what are you hiding from? Have you done
something illegal?
NORMAN: Is this a game to you, like your eyes?
HELEN: Are you a thief?
NORMAN: This is real life ya know, Helen. This is *real* life.
HELEN: I'm quite familiar with real life, "Dr. Norman."
NORMAN: Are ya really, Helen?
HELEN: So what is your real name?
NORMAN: I told ya, Norman.
HELEN: "Norman Norman?"
NORMAN: Norman Bartlamayo, okay?
HELEN: Are you on the run from someone...or something you
did?
NORMAN: All I need from you Helen is to let me stay until it
gets dark. Can ya just do that?
HELEN: Who is it you're hiding from?
NORMAN: I won't make any trouble for ya. I'll even pay ya if ya
want.

HELEN: Why are you so scared? What will happen to you if they find you?

NORMAN: If you don't want to do this for me Helen, just say so. (Norman checks window) It's not gonna be light out too much longer...

HELEN: This thing you did, ...is it bad?

NORMAN: That depends on how ya look at it.

HELEN: Did you hurt someone?

NORMAN: I took something. Okay? I took something.

HELEN: You stole something.

NORMAN: I didn't say that. I said I took something. When ya steal somethin' from somebody who's already stolen it, that's takin'...not stealin'.

HELEN: What did you "take?"

NORMAN: What do people want most in the world, Helen...what do a lot of people want in the world nowadays...more than life itself?

(Pause)

HELEN: Love?

NORMAN: *My* world Helen. Not your world, my world.

HELEN: You stole money?

NORMAN: I "took" stolen money.

HELEN: Well why? Why did you take it?

NORMAN: Because I could. Because I could take it, Helen, that's why.

HELEN: How much?

NORMAN: A lot.

(Pause)

HELEN: Well that's not right, is it?

NORMAN: What?

HELEN: Your taking something that isn't yours.

NORMAN: What's not right about it? It wasn't theirs, either. As far as the world is concerned, the money I stole... took ... shouldn't ever have existed in the first place. It's illegal. It was made by people who made it by doing illegal things, Helen. So now they don't have it anymore. I do. What's the difference?

NORMAN: (Cont) I have as much right not to have a right to have that money as they do!

HELEN: Well how do they know you have it?

NORMAN: Because they gave it to me.

HELEN: Well why would they give it to you if they didn't want you to have it?

NORMAN: They didn't give "it" to me, Helen. They gave me somethin' else that "it" was in.

HELEN: So you worked for them.

NORMAN: I ran errands for them. I was an errand boy for 'em. That's how I made my money.

HELEN: But I don't understand why they would give it to you?

NORMAN: That's exactly why, Helen. Because no one would understand why they would give it to me. Because nobody would ever suspect me of carryin' what I was carryin'. And they were right, I didn't even suspect myself of carryin' what I was carryin'...and *I* was carryin' it!

HELEN: And now they're looking for you.

NORMAN: Bingo.

HELEN: Well, why don't you just apologize to them, Norman? Explain to them that it was all a mistake. I'm sure they would understand.

(Pause)

NORMAN: Helen, I don't want you to get me wrong here, because I want you to know that I really do appreciate everything you've done for me already...that is...your not freakin' out on me here, and your not over-reacting to the situation and all that. But I do want to tell ya that I think you may not be able to truly comprehend the "dire nature" of the situation here. See it's not like I stole a towel from a hotel or somethin'.

HELEN: So these are sort of mean people that are after you, is that right, Norman?

NORMAN: Well yeah. I guess if that's the best you could do, then "mean" is a good way to describe 'em.

HELEN: Well than you should call the police.

NORMAN: I can't do that, Helen.

HELEN: Why not?

NORMAN: Because, that wouldn't be much better than having the "mean" people find out where I was.

HELEN: But if you're not one of the mean people, Norman, and the police aren't the mean people, either, then that would be two against one. You know, like two good people against one mean person... or...

NORMAN: --yeah, well I could see how you see how that makes sense, Helen, but things aren't really that clear cut anymore.

HELEN: Why not?

NORMAN: Well for one thing, I don't think the police would count me as one of the good people.

HELEN: Well, what did you do that was mean?

NORMAN: It's not so much that I did somethin' mean...it's just...well...

HELEN: --but if it's just the money you took, then you could just call the police and explain to them...

NORMAN: --it's not just the money I took, Helen.

HELEN: Well then what else?

NORMAN: It's what I did. It's what happened after I took the money.

HELEN: What did you do, Norman? Did you do something mean to someone?

NORMAN: Well see, I think to the police, it would be considered sort of mean, Helen.

HELEN: Well I don't understand. You either did something that was mean, or you didn't.

NORMAN: Why do ya think things have to be one way or the other, Helen? Sometimes you could do somethin' that's stuck right in the middle.

HELEN: In the middle of what?

NORMAN: In the middle of what a lot of people might consider "mean," and what a lot of people might consider "not mean."

HELEN: Well if something isn't mean or not mean, Norman, then what is it?

NORMAN: Then it's like what I did, Helen. It's like...it's kinda like...

HELEN: What?

NORMAN: It's like...(Norman looks toward the encyclopedias) Okay, Helen...here...(Norman goes to them) See it's kinda like your father's Encyclopedia Brittanicus's over here, okay?

HELEN: Brittanicas. Encyclopedia Brittanicas, Norman.

NORMAN: Okay, Brittania, whatever.

HELEN: What's "kinda" like it?

NORMAN: What we were talkin' about. You know, "mean" and "not mean" and "bad" and "good," and all that, okay? (He demonstrates on encyclopedias) See if "A" over here...on the left...you remember how the alphabet goes, right?

HELEN: (Indignant) Yes, Norman, even blind people can remember how the alphabet goes.

NORMAN: Okay, so if "A" is say..."good" right?...and the "Z" over here...(He breaks away) What am I doin'?

HELEN: Well finish it, Norman. You started it.

NORMAN: Alright, alright. Okay, so if "A" is good, right?

HELEN: Yes.

NORMAN: And the "Z" over here is like, bad, or meanness or whatever...than all this in between here..."B" to "Y" here... that's all different mixtures of what's caught between "A" and "Z," right? See some of these letters are closer to "A" than to "Z"...but say you're a "G" here...see? Here. (He takes her hand and has her feel how far away "G" is from "A") See how close that is away from "A?"

HELEN: Yes.

NORMAN: Well, see it's closer to "A" than to "Z," but that doesn't make it any more good than any letter not so close to "A." It just happens to be closer to "A"...or to "good," that's all. But in the wide ass scope of things, it's as much in between "A" and "Z" as anything else is.

HELEN: So in your head, the world is all in between "A" and "Z." Is that right, Norman?

NORMAN: That's right. And in your head the world is just "A" and "Z." See I don't even think there really is an "A" and "Z," Helen. I think they're just kind of mirages, ya know? To keep us all conned into believin' that maybe someday we could be one of 'em...but we can't...I don't think anybody can.

HELEN: But that's not a very positive way of looking at things, is it, Norman.

NORMAN: Well no, maybe not. But to me it's the only way of lookin' at things.

HELEN: But why can't someone be born an "A," and just never move any closer to "Z" before they die?

NORMAN: Because nobody's born an "A," Helen. Even in church, all they ever tell ya is that everybody's born a "Z," and that all life is, is one big struggle up some invisible hill to try to end up closer to "A." See I don't even believe that. I think everybody is born like a...well, like an "M," here, see? (He places her hand on "M") See that way everybody starts out with a clean slate...if you wanna go toward "Z," then you could go toward "Z." If ya wanna go toward "A," then you could go toward "A." But ya gotta do somethin'.

HELEN: Well, why can't you just stay on "M?"

NORMAN: Because, somethin' is always pullin' you the other way.

HELEN: Which other way?

NORMAN: Both other ways.

(Norman quickly takes a peek out the window)

HELEN: Well where are you now, Norman?

NORMAN: What?

HELEN: Where are you now, I mean between "A" and "Z?"

NORMAN: I think I'm as close to bein' a "Z" as you could get Helen, without actually bein' one.

HELEN: But why, what did you do that was so bad?

NORMAN: I don't want to talk about it right now, Helen, okay? All I want is for the sun to go down.

HELEN: But what happened, Norman? What did you do?

NORMAN: Just give me another half hour, that's all I'm askin'.

HELEN: You're breathing heavily again. Why are you so nervous? Why do you feel so bad inside? I could feel you feeling bad.

NORMAN: You could "feel me feeling bad?"

HELEN: That's right. I felt it with my mother too, when she was sick. Every time the pain that she felt would cut into her, I would feel it cut into me too. And I didn't mind one bit, because I kept thinking that maybe the more pain I would feel for her, the less pain she might feel for herself.

NORMAN: Well, that's really nice, Helen, but it's stupid, alright.

HELEN: No, it's not. It's the same for you. But you don't want to tell me anything.

NORMAN: I don't have to tell you anything.

HELEN: Then show me.

(Helen goes to encyclopedias)

NORMAN: What?

HELEN: Right here, on the books. (Helen puts her hand on the encyclopedias) Where am I now?

NORMAN: What are you talkin' about?

HELEN: Where is my hand, on the letters?

NORMAN: "J." Why?

HELEN: See this way I could feel how your life has gone so far, Norman.

NORMAN: What are you talkin' about?

(Helen moves her hand to the right a little)

HELEN: Here, I'm on "M" now, right? This is where you started. Now, where did you go from here?

NORMAN: What are you...?

HELEN: --after you were born on "M," Norman, which way did you go? Did you go toward "A" or "Z." Did you go toward being bad or good?

NORMAN: Hey Helen, look. Just give me a little more time here, and I'll be outa your hair, okay?

HELEN: Norman, it's the least you could do after lying to me like you did.

NORMAN: C'mon, Helen...

HELEN: --which way did you go, Norman?

NORMAN: Alright, "A," alright? I moved toward "A" after I was born...like everybody else. Nobody moves toward bein' bad, right after they're born.

HELEN: How far do you think?

NORMAN: What?

HELEN: How far do you think you moved, toward trying to be good?

NORMAN: Cripes, I don't know. "E," alright?

(Helen moves her hand to the left)

HELEN: Okay, here. Is this "E" Norman?

(He checks)

NORMAN: Yeah, yeah, it's on "E."

HELEN: Well, that's a good start. That's not a bad start at all.

NORMAN: I was just a kid.

HELEN: Then where did you go?

NORMAN: C'mon, Helen.

HELEN: It was your idea, Norman. Now, where did you go from "E." Norman!

NORMAN: "Z" I guess, alright? I moved toward "Z" after that. Everybody does when they're growin' up. It's the fashionable thing to do.

HELEN: How far?

NORMAN: I don't know. "K." Where's "K?"

(Helen moves her hand toward "Z," stopping on "K")

HELEN: Here's "K," right here. That wasn't so bad, Norman. Considering you were still just a kid, right?

NORMAN: Yeah, yeah.

HELEN: And you're still to the left of "M," aren't you?

NORMAN: Yeah, yeah, I guess.

HELEN: Now where?

NORMAN: It's all downhill from there, Helen.

HELEN: How far downhill?

NORMAN: Well wait. I did get married. So I guess that could be considered a move more in the direction of good than bad, right?

HELEN: You're married, Norman?

NORMAN: I used to be.

HELEN: Oh. Well yes, that would be counted as a good thing. How far do you think that moved you?

NORMAN: I don't know. Not much. Maybe to "I." Where's "I?"

(Helen moves her hand toward "Z," stopping on "I")

HELEN: Here. Is this it?

(He checks)

NORMAN: Yeah, yeah.

HELEN: Well that's a good move, Norman.

NORMAN: Yeah well, I thought so at the time, Helen. Believe me, it's all to the right of "M" from there.

HELEN: What happened after that?

NORMAN: A lot of things.

HELEN: Like what?

NORMAN: Like what do you think, Helen? One thing after another. What do ya think? What do ya think I came down to Atlantic City for...with the last two hundred and ten dollars I had in my life? To try to make it two hundred and ten thousand...because every time I took a step toward "A," somethin' would come along and knock me on my ass...two steps... right back toward "Z." Every time! And then when I lost that... the last money I had in the world...why do ya think I ended up gettin' involved with the kind of "mean" and "bad" people in the world that are after my ass right now? Because I wanted somethin' that I don't think I ever had the chance to have...because I wanted somethin' back...that was taken away from me...before I ever had a chance to have it. I just wanted one chance, Helen...like everybody else...just to keep my head above water. And when that was taken away from me...well than somethin' inside me just snapped, and I said to myself; "Well, to hell with it. Then I want everything now! And I don't give a crap what side of the law I have to be on to get it."

HELEN: What did you do to get it?

NORMAN: Ya can't blame a guy for gettin' "A" and "Z" mixed up nowadays, Helen. The more good I did in my life, the more bad it was for me. The more bad I did, the more good it was for me... until I started thinkin' to myself; "What exactly is so bad about bad? Bad isn't so bad. It's more good than good is."

HELEN: What did you do, Norman?

NORMAN: You can't blame anybody nowadays, Helen...

HELEN: --Norman, what is it...calm down...

NORMAN: --You can't blame me, Helen...

HELEN: --Norman, what are you talking about...

NORMAN: --I hurt somebody. (Pause) See, I hurt somebody, Helen. I didn't mean to...but I think...I hurt somebody.

HELEN: Who did you hurt?

NORMAN: One of the "mean" people.

HELEN: Well...what did you do? What did you do to him?

NORMAN: I think I sorta...I sorta shot 'im, Helen.

(Helen starts backing away from Norman)

HELEN: Well...why did you do that?

NORMAN: Because he was gonna shoot me first. How come you're movin' away like that?

HELEN: Well I think you better call the police, don't you?

NORMAN: I can't.

(Helen drifts toward phone)

HELEN: Well I think we oughta call someone, don't you think?

(Norman moves toward Helen, she backs away)

NORMAN: What are ya doin'? Stop actin' like I'm some kinda murderer or somethin'.

HELEN: Well you shouldn't be telling me things like this.

NORMAN: Helen, look. If I didn't do it to him...he was gonna do it to me. He came by my room...to do it to me.

HELEN: Well why would anyone want to hurt you, Norman?

NORMAN: Why do you think?

HELEN: The money.

NORMAN: Not to mention all the crap I have on 'em.

HELEN: Well why didn't you just give it to him? I'm sure if you explained to him that it was all some kind of misunderstanding...

NORMAN: --Helen, the guy was a killer, alright? The only thing he does all day is kill, this guy. So when he came knockin' at *my* door... the first thing I thought of, wasn't how I was gonna clear up some "misunderstanding!"

HELEN: So you shot him.

NORMAN: Not at first. I didn't have a gun. I never touched a gun in my life. I just bashed him over the head... and when he dropped his gun... I picked it up, turned around, squeezed it once and it threw me back against the wall. I was out the door before I ever got the chance to see what the hell happened.

HELEN: And then you followed me in here.

NORMAN: No, then I found Lenny.

HELEN: Who's Lenny?

NORMAN: He lives next to me at the Y. He works for 'em too.

HELEN: Well, what did he say?

NORMAN: He said I should get out of town...and away from him...because they wanted to kill me.

HELEN: Well can't he talk to them for you, Norman? Can't he help you?

NORMAN: I don't think so.

HELEN: Why not?

NORMAN: Because I have a feeling he needs more help than me right now.

HELEN: What does that mean?

NORMAN: It means the "mean" people got him. I think they thought he knew where I was.

HELEN: Well I just can't believe that these people wouldn't understand, if you just explained to them that...

NORMAN: --Helen, what kinda world do you live in here? What kinda people do ya think I'm talkin' about?

HELEN: Don't yell at me, Norman.

NORMAN: I'm sorry, Helen, alright? I've just been a little tense
    lately, okay?
(Helen moves toward phone)
HELEN: I'll call the police.
(Norman moves toward Helen, threatening)
NORMAN: We can't call the police, Helen.
HELEN: Why not!
NORMAN: Because, what do you think I'm gonna tell 'em?
HELEN: The truth. Just tell them the truth.
NORMAN: And what do you think the truth is...I mean as far as
    you see it right now?
HELEN: Well... just what you said. You got into a situation
    where you had to take a part time job working for people
    whose... whose business dealings you didn't entirely
    condone... but at the same time, you needed the work... and so
    you worked for them as an... as an errand boy... until today,
    where you happened to come across a large amount of money
    unexpectedly... and in the confusion of the situation... like
    anyone would... you seized upon the opportunity to take this
    money... and when these...these "meanies" came after you...
NORMAN: Did you just say, "meanies?"
HELEN: Yes, these...these mean people came after you...before
    you even had a chance to explain yourself to them...they...they
    tried to hurt you...
NORMAN: --kill me--
HELEN: --kill you. And so naturally you...you protected yourself
    by--
NORMAN: --trying to kill the "meanies" before they killed me.
HELEN: That's right.
NORMAN: And you think the police are gonna buy that, Helen?
HELEN: Why wouldn't they?
NORMAN: Well because for one thing, you say all that assuming
    the cops are gonna think that I'm not a "meanie" myself.
HELEN: But you're not a "meanie," Norman, you said you
    weren't.

NORMAN: Well I'm not, but it doesn't matter what I say, Helen.
And it doesn't matter what I am. It only matters what people
think I am.

HELEN: Well, what do you think people are going to think you
are?

NORMAN: What Mrs. Krazner thinks I am.

(Pause)

HELEN: Even I could see you're not "a bum," Norman, and I
can't see you.

NORMAN: Yeah well, I wish everybody could see me the way
you can't, Helen... but they can't, and so until they can, I'm
just as much a bum and a "meanie" as everybody else is. (We
hear a helicopter overhead) Great.

HELEN: What?

(Norman crosses himself)

NORMAN: If they got Lenny, he's dead now.

HELEN: How do you know?

NORMAN: Because, if they're gonna kill somebody, they're
gonna wait till Trump lands his friggin' helicopter.

HELEN: Why?

NORMAN: So nobody hears the shot.

HELEN: What do ya mean?

NORMAN: The "meanies" Helen, they have an office... a meat
locker, two blocks down from here. So if they have to kill
somebody, nobody's gonna hear them do it. We're not talkin'
highly evolved gangsters here. They haven't graduated to
silencers yet. (Norman looks out window) It won't be light out
too much longer. The longer I'm not dead, the better chance I
have of stayin' alive.

HELEN: Well, where are you going from here?

NORMAN: Out that door and into a cab...then one quick stop
before I tell the guy to drive me down to...I don't know...
Florida I guess. I don't know.

HELEN: Well I don't think you should, Norman. I think you
should turn over a new leaf... right now... and admit that
you've done wrong.

(Pause)

NORMAN: I'm sorry, what?

HELEN: Is this what you thought you'd be doing with your life when you were a little boy?

NORMAN: No, but what the hell does that have to do with anything?

HELEN: Everything. Did you think that you'd be holed up in someone's apartment in Atlantic City...and shooting people?

NORMAN: No Helen, okay? No, I didn't think that. But what about a guy who ends up sellin' insurance. Do you think he thought he was gonna end up sellin' insurance when he was a kid?

HELEN: That's not the same thing.

NORMAN: Why not?

HELEN: Because, selling insurance is honorable, compared to what you're doing. At least an insurance salesman could look at himself in the mirror every morning.

NORMAN: I could look at myself in the mirror.

(Helen points to the mirror)

HELEN: Go ahead. Look at yourself in the mirror, Norman.

NORMAN: What do *you* have a mirror for?

HELEN: It was my mother's. Go ahead, look in it.

NORMAN: I don't want to.

HELEN: Why not?

NORMAN: I just don't want to, Helen. I have other things on my mind right now, alright?

HELEN: You can't because you're ashamed of yourself, aren't you, Norman?

NORMAN: I'm not ashamed.

HELEN: You can't look at yourself because you've done wrong.

NORMAN: Hey, look, Helen...just because somebody does somethin' that's wrong nowadays, doesn't mean that it wasn't the right thing to do, okay?

HELEN: Wrong is wrong, Norman, and you know it. You're just ashamed of yourself, because you became someone to yourself that you didn't want to become.

NORMAN: Hey, I'm fine with who I am to myself.

HELEN: I don't think you like yourself, Norman. That's why you can't look yourself in the mirror right now, isn't it?

NORMAN: Hey--

HELEN: --you don't like the way you look to yourself, do you?

NORMAN: Hey... listen to me here, alright! I remember a time, believe it or not, but I remember a time when I would walk by guys that I look like now... on the street... and I used to say to myself; "to hell with them," ya know? Like I was pissed at them for not doin' what I thought was their job to do. You know, just to take care of themselves... and to get their own crap together... and to get their hands outa my face every time I walked by 'em all. And then, after what "seemed" like little thing after little thing started happening to me...after I lost *my* job...and I lost *my* wife, and *my* kids...and I started realizin' that sooner or later I'd be losin' the house that I was losin' everything in...well then I started feelin' a little less high and mighty to 'em ya know? All those hands in my face when I would walk by 'em on my way to Arby's... where I was workin' for some 18 year old pimply ass high school kid for four twenty five an hour. I mean don't get me wrong here, Helen... a lot of people with their hands in your face... askin' ya for a quarter, or five dollars, could go out there and try to get it for themselves. But after I started losin' thing after thing in my life... it started dawning on me that a lot of 'em might be more like me than I thought ...and it started makin' me nervous, ya know? How nowadays everybody's more closer to bein' the "bum on the street" than I think anybody knows. Everybody, Helen. (Pause) So don't tell me how I feel about myself, if you don't know what the hell you're talkin' about. (Pause)

HELEN: I didn't know you had children.

NORMAN: Yeah, a boy and a...a boy and a girl. (Norman takes out his weathered wallet to show Helen a picture, but then realizes what he's doing and puts the wallet back in his pocket) Listen Helen, I'm sorry. I didn't mean to yell at you or nothin'.

HELEN: I understand, Norman. (Norman checks the window)
Is it getting darker?

NORMAN: It's gettin' there Helen, it's gettin' there.

(Pause)

HELEN: What did you wanna be though, Norman, when you
were a little boy?

NORMAN: Oh, I don't know, Helen. What's the point?

HELEN: I'm just curious, that's all.

NORMAN: I don't know...somethin'. Somethin' stupid I guess,
but...

HELEN: What?

NORMAN: But...somethin' permanent, ya know? Permanent, like
my father.

HELEN: Permanent?

NORMAN: Yeah, you know... like a... like a businessman or
somethin'. Somethin' that somebody could do... that you would
know for sure that you'd be doin' the next day. Somethin'
that meant that you weren't gonna just fly off... and drift away
somewhere. Somethin' that would make ya feel like you were
attached to the ground you were walkin' on, ya know? Not like
you could just disappear, any minute... like I feel like I
could... all the time. Sometimes I feel like if it weren't for
these boots I have on, Helen... leavin' these big ass footprints,
nobody would see any traces of me anywhere at all... or like all
the ground I'm walkin' on is sand, ya know? And every time I
turn to see if there's any traces of me ever havin' walked
there... all I see is nothin'... like every time I take a step
somewhere... some kinda wind comes along and wipes all the
proof I was ever here in the first place, away... and I'm just
driftin'... (Goes to window) And I'm not the only one,
Helen. I know that. I know there's a lot of people out there
nowadays... who feel like they're hardly touchin' the ground
too. And I guess all I ever wanted when I was a kid... was the
same thing that I want now. And that's just to be able to leave
a trace of myself somewhere... permanent. Even if all it ends
up bein' is a footprint. Do ya know what I mean, Helen?

HELEN: Like Frank Sinatra...on the boardwalk, right, Norman?
NORMAN: Yeah Helen, somethin' like that. (Pause. Norman and
Helen suddenly find themselves close to each other. They
linger for an awkward moment, then Norman quickly heads for
the telephone) What's the number for a cab, do ya know?
HELEN: Why do you have to go now?
NORMAN: Because I don't wanna die, that's why.
HELEN: Well, I could make you something to eat first.
NORMAN: I can't, Helen...I'm kind of in a rush right now.
HELEN: But I like talking to you Norman, I really do.
NORMAN: Well thanks, Helen. I like talkin' to you too.
HELEN: I suppose I forgot how nice it was...talking to someone.
NORMAN: Yeah, yeah, Helen. I could see that. You should try
to get out more, ya know? Try to join some kinda club or
somethin'.
(Norman picks up the phone, dials)
HELEN: What are ya doing?
NORMAN: (In phone) Yeah, give me AC Cab, will ya?
HELEN: I could make you some meat loaf if you want...
NORMAN: (To Helen) No, that's okay, Helen. (In phone) Okay,
Thanks.
(Norman presses down on receiver and dials again)
HELEN: How about some eggs? I could make a sandwich.
NORMAN: I'm not hungry right now. (In phone) Yeah, listen. I
need a cab at uh...
HELEN: ...well then can I ask you something, Norman?
NORMAN: (To himself) Jesus, where am I?
HELEN: Would you marry me?
(Norman stops talking in phone, holds it at his side)
NORMAN: What did you just say, Helen?
HELEN: Would you marry me, Norman?
(Norman speaks into the phone again)
NORMAN: I'll call ya back. (Norman hangs up) What the hell are
ya doin', Helen?

HELEN: When you first came in here, you asked me if I was married.

NORMAN: Yeah.

HELEN: Then I asked you if you thought I was someone who could be married...and you said "yes," that you thought I was someone who could be as married as much as anyone else could.

NORMAN: Yeah.

HELEN: Well, now I'm asking if *you* would marry me...someone like you.

NORMAN: Oh, oh. You mean if...oh, okay. You mean would I...if I knew you better and all that...would I marry you?

HELEN: Yes.

NORMAN: Oh, okay, Helen. Now I know what you're talkin' about.

(Norman picks up the phone)

HELEN: Well, would you? (He dials)

NORMAN: (In phone) Yeah, it's me again...

HELEN: Norman...

NORMAN: (In phone) Hold on one second, will ya? (To Helen) Helen, just let me make one call here, okay? (In phone) Okay sorry, I need one at uh...

HELEN: Am I not what you would call "conventionally attractive?"

NORMAN: (In phone) Wait, one second. (To Helen, terse) Helen, just let me get off the phone here.

HELEN: Do you think I'm not attractive enough to get married?

NORMAN: Helen! (In phone) Alright. I need one quick, at...hello? Hey... hello? (Norman presses down on receiver) Hey!

(Norman slams down the phone)

HELEN: Well, Norman?

NORMAN: What Helen? What?

HELEN: Would you marry me?

NORMAN: Yeah, yeah. Why not? Sure, you're not bad.

HELEN: Do you mean it?

NORMAN: Yeah, why not?

(Norman reaches for phone again)

HELEN: Well, what do I look like? I don't know Norman, and I want you to tell me. I could ask Mrs. Krazner, but she wouldn't tell me the truth. (Pause) You don't have to lie.

NORMAN: Well, I don't know, Helen. How am I supposed to describe ya?

HELEN: Just tell me the truth. I'm pretty ugly, aren't I?

NORMAN: What? No, no Helen...you're not ugly. You're... no...no, not at all.

HELEN: Well...am I pretty? Don't lie, Norman.

(Pause)

NORMAN: Yeah, yeah, you're pretty. Sure. Sure you are.

(Norman reaches for phone again)

HELEN: What about my hair?

(Norman puts the phone down)

NORMAN: What about it?

HELEN: Is it still blonde? My mother's hair was the most beautiful blonde.

NORMAN: Well...that's what ya want, isn't it, Helen? You want it to be blonde, don't ya?

HELEN: Yes.

(Norman ignores her brown hair)

NORMAN: Well than you lucked out. Because it is.

HELEN: Don't lie, Norman.

NORMAN: I'm not lyin', Helen. I could see as good as you can't...and you got blonde hair, just like your mother's.

(Norman heads toward phone)

HELEN: What do you look like, Norman?

NORMAN: Helen, you don't want to know.

HELEN: You sound very handsome.

NORMAN: Oh...well, no. I wouldn't say that...good lookin' yeah, you know, if I scrubbed myself up a little bit...but, I wouldn't say handsome.

HELEN: I bet you are.

NORMAN: Oh no...well, maybe.

HELEN: What kind of clothes do you have on?

NORMAN: Well, uh...the usual, I guess.

HELEN: A suit?

NORMAN: A suit? Well, yeah, you know...sort of...

HELEN: I wish I could see you, Norman. I bet your wife is beating herself over the head, wishing she could have you back.

NORMAN: Oh, I wouldn't be too sure about that, Helen.

(Norman reaches for phone)

HELEN: And I bet even with all this happening...your children would be very proud of you.

NORMAN: What?

HELEN: Your children, Norman. I bet they would be very proud of you. (Norman is frozen. He glances toward the mirror, catching himself in it. At first he makes a conscious effort to avoid it, but then finds himself gravitating toward it, mesmerized. He goes to it, wipes away some dust covering it and stares at his reflection) Norman? Norman... (Norman breaks away from his reflection and heads toward the window, looking out. After a pause, Helen speaks...softly...) Is it dark out yet?

NORMAN: Almost, Helen.

HELEN: I wonder if the sun will shine red tonight, before it sets?

NORMAN: I couldn't tell ya.

(Norman takes out his wallet again, looks at the picture)

HELEN: I suppose I miss them more than I thought I would... sunsets I mean.

NORMAN: Yeah well, you oughta do somethin' about that. (Pause. Norman quickly glances at the picture) And you're wrong ya know. They wouldn't be proud of me... they'd be ashamed.

HELEN: You don't know that, Norman.

NORMAN: Yeah, I do. They'd be ashamed.

(Norman puts the picture and his wallet back in his pocket. He goes to the phone again, picking up the receiver)

HELEN: Would you like to hear a joke, Norman...before you go?

NORMAN: What?

HELEN: A joke. Would you like to hear a joke?

NORMAN: (Holding phone) No, Helen, not now!

HELEN: Well alright, then fine.

(Pause. Helen, dejected, moves away from Norman, who dials a couple numbers, looks toward Helen, dials a couple more, then finally gives in and hangs up the phone)

NORMAN: Alright, alright, Helen. Go ahead. Tell me your joke, but make it quick.

HELEN: Okay. Well see it isn't even so much an actual joke really, as it is just something I think is kind of funny.

NORMAN: Well, what? What!?

HELEN: Well...when I was a little girl, I was afraid of the dark. (Helen laughs to herself a little. Pause)

NORMAN: So?

HELEN: So...isn't that sort of funny...I mean, being that I'm blind now?

NORMAN: Well...no, not really. And it especially isn't funny bein' that you volunteered to be blind now.

HELEN: Yes, but isn't it ironic in a way. I mean someone being scared of something all their life...and then in the end, having to end up living with it...all their life?

NORMAN: Oh, yeah, Helen. That's a regular laugh riot. (Norman heads for phone)

HELEN: And do you want to hear something even funnier, Norman?

NORMAN: What Helen...what?!

HELEN: I'm not scared of it anymore. The dark, I mean.

NORMAN: Well...isn't that all you could see now, Helen...dark?

HELEN: Yes, but that's what I want you to understand, Norman. I don't see the darkness in the same way anymore. It's not that scary to me. It's not the kind of darkness where I feel like I don't know where everything is. It's the kind of darkness that you could trust, as much as you could trust anything that you can't see.

NORMAN: Ya can't trust anything ya can't see, Helen.

(As Helen recites the following speech, she slips into a kind of trance. Norman watches her as she talks, but then gradually begins to feel haunted himself, sensing a presence in the room somewhere. He is uneasy for a moment, then directs his attention back to Helen)

HELEN: I know it sounds silly, Norman. I don't know how else to explain it... except to say that it's the same darkness that I remember as a child... when my mother would come upstairs... to my room... and she would sit on the side of my bed and hum something... I couldn't hum it again if I wanted to... I forgot what it sounded like I suppose. But she would hum it, and while she was doing that, she would stroke my hair... and all this time I wouldn't be able to see her... and I remember feeling like I couldn't be happier... I couldn't feel more safe than when she was doing that... but if I would say something... I remember if I would say something... (Pause) "Helen," she would say. "Shh... go to sleep now... go to sleep..." and I would reach... (Pause) And I would reach...

(Norman senses a presence in the room)

NORMAN: Do you feel like you can see her now, Helen? (Pause) Helen!

(Helen emerges)

HELEN: Yes, Norman?

NORMAN: Your mother isn't here anymore, Helen. Your mother is dead. Your mother is dead.

HELEN: Oh I know, Norman, I know. (Pause) Well, you have to go now, I know.

(Pause. Norman walks toward phone, then turns)

NORMAN: That's why ya did it, isn't it, Helen?

HELEN: What?

NORMAN: Let yourself go blind like ya did. Because you knew as long as you couldn't see the things ya still wanted to see, there would always be the chance that they still might be there. Isn't that right?

HELEN: I think you better call your cab, Norman.

(Pause)

NORMAN: Okay, Helen. Okay. (Norman goes to the phone, picks up the receiver, looks toward Helen, dials a couple numbers, looks toward Helen again, then slams the phone down, hard) Damnit!

HELEN: What?

NORMAN: You gotta do somethin', Helen.

HELEN: About what?

NORMAN: Of all the friggin' houses.

HELEN: What are you talking about?

NORMAN: The way you're livin', Helen. And this place you're livin' in. It's not normal and it's not healthy. Damnit!

HELEN: Why not?

NORMAN: Because *you* did wrong too, Helen. To yourself. You did wrong to yourself as much as I did to anybody else.

HELEN: What do you mean?

NORMAN: Your eyes, Helen! What do you think I mean? Your not being able to "seeness." Ya gotta take care of that. You're still young, ya know, ya can't...ya can't do what you did. It's not right.

HELEN: What's not right about it?

NORMAN: It's wrong, that's all. I mean here I am, bustin' my ass so I could keep my eyes open, and you go ahead and just pull the plug on yours...voluntarily! That's not right.

HELEN: Well, it's what...

NORMAN: --and what *about* your mother?

HELEN: What about her?

NORMAN: Do ya think she'd be happy about the way you're livin' now?

HELEN: I really don't see how that...

NORMAN: --she didn't go ahead and pull the plug on *her*self, did she?

HELEN: She couldn't. She couldn't move, Norman.

NORMAN: But she could scream. She could scream at least. Ya said that, didn't ya?

HELEN: She couldn't scream. She couldn't make a sound.

NORMAN: Well then she screamed even if nobody could hear her... like most people do. But at least she did somethin'... at least she fought back somehow against all the bad and all the pain that was killin' her. She didn't just sit here like a coward, and watch the life she had... even if it wasn't so great, fade out, inch by inch, like you're doin'... livin' in some kinda dream world, where all ya have to do is poke your own eyes out and pretend that everything's not that bad at all... and not because it isn't that bad... but just because ya can't see it is! (Pause)

HELEN: Call your cab, Norman.

NORMAN: Don't ya wanna see again, Helen?

HELEN: You better call now.

NORMAN: Wouldn't ya wanna see if ya could? And ya could, couldn't ya?

(Helen heads toward the kitchen)

HELEN: I'll make you a sandwich, Norman.

NORMAN: Helen!

HELEN: What!

NORMAN: I just think...look, I'm not anybody to you, but I just think that if ya could...if you could get yourself somehow to see someday... then ya should. That's all I'm sayin'.

HELEN: Why Norman? Why are you saying that?

NORMAN: Because you could see what most people can't anyway, Helen. So you might as well see what they can. (Pause) I'm just tryin' to give ya a compliment here, that's all. (Pause)

HELEN: Thank you, Norman.

(Norman finds himself very close to Helen now, awkward, but he doesn't move away)

NORMAN: Yeah, well, ya know...no problem, Helen. No problem. (They gravitate toward each other a little closer) Well, I guess uh...

HELEN: Yes, well...

(The doorbell rings. Norman and Helen don't hear it. They move closer to each other, about to kiss. The doorbell rings again. Norman hears it; looks toward the door)

NORMAN: Shit.

(Norman breaks away from Helen)

HELEN: What is it?

(Norman takes his gun out and points it toward the door)

NORMAN: (Whispering) Quiet.

HELEN: Should I ask who it is?

NORMAN: Get away from the door!

HELEN: Who do you think it is, Norman?

NORMAN: I don't know, Helen. Wait.

(Pause. Silence)

HELEN: They're gone.

NORMAN: Wait...(Three hard knocks at the door) Get behind the sofa!

HELEN: Why do I...

NORMAN: --get down!

(Helen finds her way behind the sofa. Norman gets on his knees, behind the stair railing and points his gun toward the door. The doorknob turns several times, then we hear a key key in the door. It gradually begins to open. Slowly emerging is Mrs. Krazner, with a bowling ball in one hand, a cup of sugar in the other. Norman quickly puts away his gun)

MRS. KRAZNER: (Whispering) Helen?

(Helen jumps up from behind the couch)

HELEN: Mrs. Krazner!

MRS. KRAZNER: (Startled) Oh my God...Helen, what are you doin' down there? (Mrs. Krazner turns and sees Norman. As soon as she does, she begins to swing her bowling ball toward him in a threatening manner) Alright Mister, hold it right there...show's over Mister wise aleck!

NORMAN: What the hell are you doin'?

MRS. KRAZNER: (Swinging ball) Just keep your distance!

HELEN: Mrs. Krazner, what's going on?

NORMAN: (Dodging about) She's gonna throw a bowling ball at me, Helen!

HELEN: Mrs. Krazner!

MRS. KRAZNER: Call the police, Helen...

NORMAN: Hey, Mrs. Krazner, watch that thing will ya, you're gonna hurt somebody here!
(Mrs. Krazner continues swinging the bowling ball, becoming more and more exhausted)

MRS. KRAZNER: You just freeze right there, Mister! (Mrs. Krazner's face contorts in agony) Oh my God!

HELEN: What's the matter?

MRS. KRAZNER: Oh my God! (Mrs. Krazner stops swinging the bowling ball and collapses in a chair, her arm hanging over the side of it, with the bowling ball resting on the floor) Oh God, my arm socket! Somethin' tore outa my socket! My arm tore outa my socket!

HELEN: Mrs. Krazner...

NORMAN: Well what the hell do you expect? You're an old lady for Cripes sake!

HELEN: What do you have a bowling ball for, Mrs. Krazner?

MRS. KRAZNER: I wasn't gonna take any chances! What has he done to you, Helen? What has he done?

HELEN: He hasn't done anything, Mrs. Krazner, honestly. We were just talking, that's all.

NORMAN: In all the time I've been here Mrs. Krazner, I haven't touched a hair on anybody's head. And in that same time, you've tried to kill me with a phone...and then bowl me to death. Now who shouldn't trust who here?

HELEN: I'm fine, Mrs. Krazner. I really am, I promise. (Pause)

MRS. KRAZNER: You need somebody to look out for you Helen, that's all.

HELEN: I know, Mrs. Krazner, I know.

NORMAN: Maybe she could look out for herself better than you think.

MRS. KRAZNER: How would you know?

HELEN: Thank you for dropping by, Mrs. Krazner.

MRS. KRAZNER: What are you gonna have for supper, Helen?

HELEN: Oh, I have some chicken.

MRS. KRAZNER: Well do ya want me to put it in for ya?

HELEN: No, I'll be fine. Really.

(Mrs. Krazner gets up with her bowling ball)

MRS. KRAZNER: Well, alright. I better get back...make sure those gas men don't come without my bein' there. Oh yeah, here's your sugar.

(Puts sugar on table)

HELEN: What gas men, Mrs. Krazner?

MRS. KRAZNER: The gas men...comin' to check on the meters. Mrs. O'Sullivan saw 'em comin' down this way.

HELEN: But we just had our meters read three days ago.

MRS. KRAZNER: Well, she said they have to do it again...they made some kind of mistake or somethin'. She said they've been up and down the street all day.

NORMAN: How many gas men are there?

MRS. KRAZNER: Two. One for each side of the street.

HELEN: Why would they come this late?

(Norman peeks out window)

NORMAN: Where are they now, Mrs. Krazner?

MRS. KRAZNER: What do you care?

HELEN: I care, Mrs. Krazner. Where are they?

MRS. KRAZNER: I don't know. A block down I guess. How am I supposed to know everything?

NORMAN: Great.

MRS. KRAZNER: (To Norman) What's the matter with you?

HELEN: Nothing, Mrs. Krazner. Thank you again for dropping by.

MRS. KRAZNER: Are you sure you don't...

HELEN: --I'm sure. (Helen leads her out) You better get back.

MRS. KRAZNER: Well, just call me if you need anything, dear.

HELEN: I will, thank you very much, Mrs. Krazner. Thank you. Goodbye. (Helen shuffles Mrs. Krazner out the door, closing it hard behind her. She turns to Norman, who has begun to pace frantically) Do you think it's the meanies, Norman?

NORMAN: Yeah, I do, Helen.

HELEN: Well, what are we going to do?

NORMAN: I don't know yet, I'm thinkin' here.

HELEN: Well do you want me to do something?

NORMAN: No, Helen, just wait a minute.

HELEN: You're breathing heavily again, Norman.

NORMAN: Just be quiet a second, will ya?

(Suddenly Norman stops pacing, having again caught his reflection in the mirror. He freezes, staring at it for some time)

HELEN: What is it, Norman, what are you doing?

NORMAN: You're right ya know, Helen.

HELEN: About what?

NORMAN: I did do wrong. I did do wrong, Helen. (Pause. Norman reaches into his pocket and takes out a key) I need you to do somethin' for me.

HELEN: What?

(He walks the key over to a small vase on the table)

NORMAN: You know this vase, over here, by the stairs?

HELEN: Yes, why?

NORMAN: I'm droppin' a key inside.

(He drops the key)

HELEN: What for?

NORMAN: Because you have to do me a favor.

HELEN: What, Norman?

NORMAN: I'm gonna have to leave soon.

HELEN: Where are you going?

NORMAN: I'm not sure yet, Helen, but I need you to do somethin' for me, after I'm gone.

HELEN: What?

NORMAN: Do you remember where the train station is?

HELEN: If it hasn't moved.

(Norman holds Helen by the shoulders, tight)

NORMAN: It hasn't. Now listen to me, Helen, and don't forget a thing I say.

HELEN: I won't.

NORMAN: After I leave--

HELEN: --but--

NORMAN: --listen, Helen! After I leave, I need you to go to the station for me.

HELEN: What for?

NORMAN: To get somethin' for me.

HELEN: Where?

NORMAN: In one of the lockers there. That's why you're gonna need the key.

HELEN: Alright.

NORMAN: Now, the locker number is 381. Can you remember that?

HELEN: 381.

NORMAN: Okay, Good. Now, here's the thing; I want you to wait fifteen, no, five minutes after I leave this place here, and then I want you to go to The Thunderbird Hotel for the night, and ask for a guy named Fritz. You take a cab. Tell 'im you're a friend of mine, and he'll give you a decent room. Then, if I don't get in touch with you sometime tonight, I want you to take what's in the locker there tomorrow, and I want you to keep it for yourself, but you can't come back here. Helen, you can not come back here.

HELEN: But what--

NORMAN: --hang on, Helen. Here's how ya do it. You take what's in the plastic bag, there in the locker, and you split it in half...and you take one half to one bank--

HELEN: --oh, no I couldn't--

NORMAN: --wait, Helen...and ya take the other half to another. And at both banks, you tell them that you inherited what you brought to them there... from your mother... and if they ask anymore questions beyond that... you just tell them that you found it in a closet somewhere... in this place... but you don't tell them the truth. Do you understand what I'm sayin' here, Helen... you don't tell them the truth.

HELEN: But, Norman, I can't--

NORMAN: (Terse) --Helen! Just listen to me here, okay! Now, after that, you wait two days... and then you take out whatever you need, and you say goodbye to your mother, and then you say goodbye to Mrs. Krazner, and you say goodbye to this whole friggin' place, but you don't come back here. Ever! Do you understand that, Helen? (Pause) And then you take out whatever else you need... you take out whatever else you need...

HELEN: ...what...?

NORMAN: (Almost threatening) ...and you get your eyes fixed. (Pause) Do you understand what I'm sayin' to you here? You get your eyes fixed.

HELEN: But Norman, I couldn't--

NORMAN: (Terse) --be quiet, Helen.

HELEN: But Norman, I--

NORMAN: (Exploding) --HELEN, SHUT UP! (Pause. Norman regains his composure) Helen, you have to do what I say. You don't understand, but if you don't do what I say you're gonna end up makin' my life less worth it than it already is. Do you understand what I'm sayin' here Helen? (Helen is frozen, looking away. Suddenly there are three hard knocks on the door. Norman takes out his gun and points it toward the door. Pause. Three hard knocks again, followed by a voice: "Gas man!" Norman quickly goes to Helen and whispers in her ear...) Get in the kitchen.

HELEN: But--

NORMAN: --go! (Leading her in) And don't come out 'til I tell ya to.

(Norman forcibly guides Helen into the kitchen. He returns and faces the door, his gun pointed toward it. We hear a voice call "Gas man" again and three hard knocks. Norman gets low and scrambles over to the lamp, which he turns off. The room is in semi- darkness now, only a little light from the streetlight coming through the window. We see Norman's silhouette walking toward the front door, slowly, with his gun in his hand. Norman is still for a moment, frozen. Faintly, we see a

(Cont) figure slowly emerging from the darkness, behind Norman, coming down the stairs and making its way toward the center of the living room. Norman turns around startled and whispers into the darkness; "Helen?"..."Helen, what are you doin'?" In one instant, the lamp is switched on and standing next to it is Pauly, a very large man with a gun in his hand pointed directly at Norman. Norman is facing Pauly as well, with his gun pointed directly at him. They stand there, squared off)

PAULY: Hey, Norman, how ya doin'?

NORMAN: Hey, Pauly.

PAULY: You killed Frank, Norman.

NORMAN: I didn't mean to, Pauly.

PAULY: Yeah, but now everybody's *really* mad at you.

NORMAN: Well yeah, but see I didn't mean to. He was a scumbag, you know that, Pauly.

PAULY: Yeah, I know.

NORMAN: What happened to Lenny?

PAULY: Oh, he's fine, Norman. He's just dead, that's all. Isn't that Frank's gun?

NORMAN: Yeah, why?

PAULY: Well than there's no more bullets in it...are there?

NORMAN: Sure there are. Sure there are, Pauly. What are you talkin' about?

(Pauly starts moving toward Norman)

PAULY: I don't think so, Norman. Because Frank used to only use one on a job. Don't ya remember? He used to brag about that all the time.

NORMAN: No, no, Pauly. There's another bullet in here.

(Pauly lets down his gun as he slowly approaches Norman)

PAULY: Then how come you're not shootin' me, Norman, when I'm walkin' up to you like this?

NORMAN: (Backing up) I'm waiting for you to get closer, that's all.

(Pauly puts out his hand as he approaches Norman)

PAULY: Give me the gun, Norman.

(Norman takes aim at Pauly's head)

NORMAN: I don't want to do this, Pauly.

PAULY: Give me the gun. (Pauly stops in front of Norman and sticks his hand out again. Pause. Norman slowly lowers his gun and places it in Pauly's hand. Pauly then takes the gun, puts it up to Norman's head and squeezes it off, six times in quick succession) You're such a dickhead, Norman.

HELEN: (From kitchen) Norman?

NORMAN: Stay there!

PAULY: Does she know where the money is, Norman?

NORMAN: She doesn't know shit. She's just some blind bitch I followed home.

PAULY: All they want is for you to be dead. I could do that. I could do that for them. Or maybe you and I could work somethin' out.

NORMAN: Like what?

PAULY: Like you give me the money...and I tell them you're dead.

NORMAN: Or...

PAULY: Or...you don't give me the money, and I show them that you're dead.

NORMAN: But that's kinda breakin' the rules, isn't it, Pauly?

PAULY: Well you know me, Norman...I'm like you...I've always been sort of an entrepreneur at heart.

NORMAN: They didn't have to kill Lenny.

PAULY: They don't have to do a lot of things, Norman.

NORMAN: They're scumbags.

PAULY: Where is it?

HELEN: (From kitchen) Norman?

PAULY: Don't be stupid.

HELEN: (From kitchen) Norman!

NORMAN: (To Helen) STAY THERE!

(Pauly raises the gun to Norman's temple)

PAULY: Yes or no Norman, c'mon.

HELEN: (From kitchen) Norman!

PAULY: Three seconds, Norman, yes or no.

NORMAN: Pauly...
PAULY: Three...
HELEN: (From kitchen) Norman!
PAULY: Two...
NORMAN: Pauly...
PAULY: One. (Pauly cocks the gun, pressing it hard against
   Norman's head) Do ya really wanna die a bum, Norman?
NORMAN: What did you just say?
PAULY: Do ya really wanna die a bum?
HELEN: (From kitchen) Norman!
NORMAN: It's alright, Helen! Stay there! (To himself) It's
   alright.
   (Pressing the gun harder against Norman's head)
PAULY: What do ya say, Norman? What do ya say?
   (Pause. Norman is frozen for a moment. Then he looks toward
   the kitchen door, then straight into Pauly's face)
NORMAN: Well, what else can I say, Pauly? What else can I
   say? (Pause) Fuck you. Fuck you, Pauly, and I'm not a bum.
   (Pauly strikes Norman across the face with his gun, sending him
   down, behind the couch. Helen bursts out of the kitchen)
HELEN: Norman!
   (Norman struggles to get up, bloodied)
NORMAN: It's alright, Helen. It's alright.
PAULY: Hello, Helen.
HELEN: Who are you?
NORMAN: He's my ride Helen. He's my taxi.
PAULY: Yeah, that's right. Very nice to meet you, Helen.
HELEN: What's going on?
NORMAN: I gotta go now, Helen.
HELEN: Where...where are you going?
PAULY: I'll take care of him, Helen. Don't worry about it.
   (Pauly goes to Norman, takes hold of him hard around his neck,
   puts the gun to his head and starts leading him out the door)
NORMAN: It'll be alright, Helen.

(Pauly opens the door, leading Norman out)

HELEN: Wait...Norman.

NORMAN: Everything's alright, Helen, don't worry about it.

HELEN: Norman...

PAULY: Nice meeting you, Helen.

HELEN: Wait...Norman. Will I see you again?

(Norman forces Pauly to stop)

NORMAN: That depends Helen. You tell me. Will you "see" me?

HELEN: What?

NORMAN: Will you "see" me, Helen? Will ya "see" me?

(Pause, Helen realizes...)

HELEN: Yes! Yes Norman, I will. I will "see" you.

NORMAN: Well that's good, Helen. That's real good.

(Pauly jerks Norman through the front door and into the night, slamming the door behind them)

HELEN: Norman?

(Helen runs toward the door, stopping just in front of it. She freezes for a moment. Slowly, we begin to hear the faint ticking of the formerly broken clock. Helen turns toward it. Touches it. She stands there with her hand on the clock, as we begin to hear the distant sound of the approaching whirly-bird. It's loudness and intensity rises to a full crescendo as Helen looks up slightly, and the lights fade slowly to black)

THE END

BILLY AND DAGO

"Billy and Dago" was first produced in a workshop at The Yale School of Drama with the following cast:

Billy: Tom Beckett
Dago: William Francis McGuire

The director was Elizabeth Margid.

The play was given its first professional production at The Angel Theatre, New York City with:

Billy: Scott Cohen
Dago: Peter Gregory

The director was Anastasia Traina.

The play was then featured in The Actors Studio One Act Festival at The Actors Studio, New York City with:

Billy: Damian Young
Dago: Peter Gregory

The director was Rob Greenberg.

The play was given its Los Angeles premier at The Flight Theatre with:

Billy: Shane Patrick McCullough
Dago: Peter Gregory

The director was Charles Evered.

"Billy and Dago" was inspired by the short story; "An Old Time Raid," by William Carlos Williams. The author would like to thank The Williams Estate for their kind permission and support.

For William Carlos Williams

The Characters

BILLY MANNING: Late twenties, thirties

DAGO SCHULTZ: Late twenties, thirties

The setting and Time

The play takes place in Billy's office in New York City.

The time is the present.

(As the lights come up we see a well dressed Billy at his desk. He looks at his watch, gets up, walks to the window. He spots something, goes about the room messing things up, including his own desk. He sits down again, tries to act as if he's hard at work. Dago enters, dressed like a modern hobo, with a cigarette dangling from his mouth)

DAGO: I couldn't believe it. "He's a salesman in New York City."

BILLY: Dago...

DAGO: I had to make an appointment to see ya.

BILLY: Well God, it's been awhile.

DAGO: If there was one thing each of us would never be, it was "somebody who somebody else had to make an appointment to see."

BILLY: Where the hell have you been?

DAGO: I'd be stupid for me to even try and tell ya, except to say this; that I never know where I'm goin' till I get there, since by the time I get to a place I'm broke, and as a result of that I'm sober, and one of the worst things about bein' sober is that you know where you are. What are you doin' here?

BILLY: Whatdoya mean?

DAGO: I can't believe it.

BILLY: It's been a few years, ya know?

DAGO: Yeah but Billy, a tie? Shoes like that?

BILLY: So where the hell have ya been? The last time I saw you was--

DAGO: --comin' back from Passaic.

BILLY: Yeah, and you jumped on that freight.

DAGO: The one we thought was movin'.

BILLY: Yeah, we were walkin' by it, and since we were movin', it looked like it was.

DAGO: It was.

BILLY: No it wasn't. It only looked that way 'cause we were walkin' next to it. We were blitzed.

DAGO: C'mon Billy, lets jump it!

BILLY: It's not movin'!

DAGO: So I jump on it like an asshole, and I finally see it isn't movin', and as soon as I see it isn't movin', it starts to. Billy it's movin! Billy!

BILLY: Dago get off it!

DAGO: Billy! Get on! Get on!

BILLY: God that was funny.

DAGO: Oh yeah, hilarious. So I pass out on it and end up in Philadelphia.

BILLY: Get out.

DAGO: Yup

BILLY: How long were ya down there?

DAGO: I just got back.

BILLY: No way!

DAGO: Yup. I couldn't think of anything else to do, so I just stayed. God, that's pretty sad.

BILLY: Who did ya know down there?

DAGO: Whoever I met. How does a guy get into...what do you do?

BILLY: I'm a buyer...wholesale.

DAGO: Oh yeah. How does a guy get into that?

BILLY: Well, it's like anything else.

DAGO: What about...I thought you wanted to...

BILLY: Well, you know, in college I did communications and stuff.

DAGO: Yeah.

BILLY: And uhm, it's really all a part of that. It's all in the same spectrum really.

DAGO: Whatdoya mean?

BILLY: Well...

DAGO: I thought you wanted to be a sports announcer guy.

BILLY: Well yeah.

DAGO: Like Howard Cosell or somethin'.

BILLY: Yeah, that's what I'm talkin' about.

DAGO: Well how is that like this?

BILLY: Well you know, ya get out in the field, and ya see a lot of these things are really, in a way, kind of related. Like sportscasting even. It's all about getting things across. You know, you see things, you analyze 'em, and then you tell 'em to other people. That's what communication is... which isn't far from what I do.

DAGO: How is that?

BILLY: Well, that's what I do. I look over things for a store... and then I kinda analyze 'em. And then I communicate it with the store... as to whether or not they should buy it. (Pause)

DAGO: Oh.

BILLY: So it all... you know, it sounds different, but whenever ya break somethin' down to the bone, ya see it's all the same thing really. Communications, sportscasting, wholesale clothes. You know, whatever.

DAGO: Yeah.

BILLY: Yeah, it's all in the same ballpark really. And ya know, actually, come to think of it... if you plan on stayin' around awhile, I might be able to hook you up with somethin'. You'd have to start ground floor, but...

DAGO: So now this is what you do?

BILLY: Yeah. You know, for now. It's a start.

DAGO: Yeah.

BILLY: I mean I only got it 'cause a friend of mine has a father who was talkin' to me about shit, and uhm, you know, I mean I went out and I went for interviews and stuff... I sent out all those resumes, but I don't think my school was big enough. I mean broadcasting is a tough nut to crack like anything else. You know, ya gotta know somebody. So, I talk to this guy's father and he says he's got this job... and I figure, you know, till I crack the nut. There's just so many people for so many jobs, and I figure I might as well do somethin' till I figure out what I'm doin'. Or you know, till things thin out a little.

DAGO: Yeah. (Pause) What things though?

BILLY: You know, till I get some bucks under my belt and uhm... I still keep watchin' the games and stuff, readin' the papers for stats. It's not like I don't do anything having to do with it anymore. I just figure, till the right time comes... this is okay. For now.

DAGO: Yeah?

BILLY: Yeah. (Now sure) Yeah. (Pause)

DAGO: Well, you strike me as the kinda guy you and me used to like to hate, Billy.

BILLY: Whatdoya mean?

DAGO: Nothin'.

BILLY: What?

DAGO: Nothin'. (Dago wanders to the window and looks out) I went by home.

BILLY: Where, Paterson?

DAGO: No, Beverly fuckin' Hills. Yeah, Paterson.

BILLY: Who'd ya see, anybody?

DAGO: Yeah, I saw your mom.

BILLY: How's she doin'?

DAGO: Okay. When's the last time ya saw her?

BILLY: I don't know. You know, new job. I don't know.

DAGO: What is she, seven hundred miles away?

BILLY: I just never have the time. I call her.

DAGO: Can't you make the time?

BILLY: It's not a matter of that. It just never...jells really.

DAGO: It never what?

BILLY: Jells. It's--

DAGO: --what the fuck is that?

BILLY: It's just a way of saying things don't come together.

DAGO: What is this with words lately? Everybody's sayin' everything as little as possible.

BILLY: It's just a word. I'll see her. You know, our times just haven't criss-crossed in a good enough way for it to happen yet.

DAGO: God, you're startin' to sound like ya look.

BILLY: Whatdoya mean?

DAGO: I mean all slick and stuff.

BILLY: Well...

DAGO: I went to see my mom too.

BILLY: Oh yeah?

DAGO: Yeah, it was stupid. I mean I looked all over, I couldn't find 'er. I mean I went there, but I forgot where she was. I remembered her being by a tree, but I forgot there were so many trees there. So I tried to look at every one... but the place was too big and it was gettin' dark and I felt stupid. So, I just put some flowers on some lady's that had the same first name as her. (Pause) A grave's a grave. It doesn't make any difference.

BILLY: No, it doesn't.

DAGO: It's the idea that counts.

BILLY: Yeah. (Pause) Did you see your...

DAGO: No, I went by Hub's for the fuck of it. Just to see if he was there. He wasn't. I mean I figured that, figurin' he's probably dead somewhere, drunk off his ass. So I sat down and just ordered one up and uh... Hub turns to me and goes..."Not on your life ya welcher." I go "Hub, it's me" and he goes "Get your ass outa here before I call the cops." I go "Hub, it's me, Dago." And he comes closer and looks at me and tilts my head in the light and starts apologizin' 'cause he thought... I think he thought I was my old man. Jesus. Then he buys me one on the house to make up for it. Christ. (Pause) Anyway, I still owe ya ten bucks.

BILLY: From what?

DAGO: From somethin' I forget. But I just remembered.

(Dago reaches in his pocket)

BILLY: No, don't. If ya pay me back I won't see ya again.

DAGO: What?

BILLY: I mean if you still owe it to me, there's always the chance I might see ya again.

(Dago smiles, puts money away)

DAGO: Alright, whatever. I'm not welchin' on ya though.

BILLY: I know.

(Pause. Dago goes to the window, then turns and delivers
softly)

DAGO: Let's go Billy.

BILLY: Where?

DAGO; Anywhere but here.

BILLY: What are you talkin' about?

DAGO: I'm talkin' about gettin' outa here.

BILLY: What, for lunch?

DAGO: No. For good.

BILLY: What are you talkin' about?

DAGO: I'm talkin' about you and me, right now, not bein' here
anymore. I'm talkin' about goin' back home and catchin' a fast
one up north.

BILLY: A train?

DAGO: Yeah.

BILLY: Don't even kid around.

DAGO: I'm not, let's go.

BILLY: I'm workin' here.

DAGO: So what?

BILLY: I'm not sayin' I can't do it. I'm just sayin' I don't wanna.

DAGO: Billy...

BILLY: There's a difference.

DAGO: Billy this office. I mean it's alright, but it's kinda small
isn't it? I mean it's kinda cramped in here. Don't you feel that?

BILLY: I don't know.

DAGO: Alright, then if ya don't wanna jump trains with me, let's
at least get drunk.

BILLY: I'm workin' here.

DAGO: Billy c'mon. Everywhere I go to see somebody, they're
either not there, or they're so different that they might as well
not be.

BILLY: Well it's been awhile.

DAGO: One drink.

BILLY: I can't.

DAGO: Billy...

BILLY: I can't.

(Dago makes his way to Billy's desk and notices his stationary)

DAGO: Wow. "William F. Manning." Now this, having your name on something like this, this is impressive Billy.

BILLY: Everybody has it done.

DAGO: Not everybody. I don't.

BILLY: I mean you know, the company does it.

DAGO: "William F. Manning." What does the "F" stand for?

BILLY: Francis.

DAGO: Oh yeah, your dad.

BILLY: Yeah.

DAGO: How's he doin'?

BILLY: He's alright.

DAGO: He dried out?

BILLY: Yeah, once in awhile he's dry.

DAGO: That's good. Is he still livin' at home?

BILLY: Once in awhile I guess.

DAGO: When he's dry.

BILLY: Yeah.

DAGO: All through school we only talked about three things you and me. Girls, our drunk fathers, and girls.

BILLY: Yeah.

DAGO: (Looking at stationary) "William F. Manning." What do you think *my* real name is Billy?

BILLY: God, I never... I don't know, what is it?

DAGO: No I mean really. I'm askin' you. Take a guess.

BILLY: I don't know, what is it?

DAGO: No I mean I really don't know.

BILLY: What's Dago?

DAGO: Do you think that's my real name?

BILLY: I don't know, didn't your parents ever tell ya?

DAGO: No, they just called me Dago.

BILLY: Then I guess that's it. Look on your birth certificate.

DAGO: I never saw mine.

BILLY: Well, where were ya born?

DAGO: I don't know. I don't remember.

BILLY: Well what does it say on your other stuff?

DAGO: Like what?

BILLY: Social Security, all that.

DAGO: I don't know. I don't have any of that.

BILLY: What do ya have with your name on it?

DAGO: Nothin'.

BILLY: Bullshit.

DAGO: No, I don't have anything with my name on it.

BILLY: Why not?

DAGO: I don't know. I never needed it.

BILLY: What about for jobs?

DAGO: Everybody whoever paid me anything, paid me in cash.

BILLY: What about school?

DAGO: Everybody called me Dago, or "asshole" in school. I was never officially in classes anyway.

BILLY: Whatdoya mean?

DAGO: I was always in the principal's office.

BILLY: I know.

DAGO: Yeah, but not just for what I did. I remember every year they'd call me down and ask me where my parents were, and over and over again I'd tell 'em, "My mother's dead and my father's away on business."

BILLY: Was he?

DAGO: Yeah, right. He was at Hub's gettin' crocked. And then they'd tell me to tell my parents to get my papers, so they could prove who I am. Why do ya have to prove somebody's who they are? Isn't them sittin' right in front of ya enough to prove who they are? If they weren't who they were, why would they be sittin' right in front of ya in the first place?

BILLY: I can't believe you got nothin' on ya.

DAGO: The way I figure it, the one good thing about not havin' all that I.D. shit, is that it keeps ya from existing too much.

BILLY: What?

DAGO: Existing too much. It's philosophical.

BILLY: Oh.

DAGO: Once you have your name all over everything, you're dead in the water. See you exist too much "William F. Manning." I'd rather be who I am, even if I don't know exactly who that is.

BILLY: Jesus.

(Dago walks around the office)

DAGO: Are you tellin' me you don't feel like these walls are closin' in on ya?

BILLY: I told ya, nothing I'm doing is forever.

DAGO: Yeah, but all the time you're thinkin' that way, you could end up doin' the same thing... forever.

BILLY: (Turning away) So who'd ya see back home?

DAGO: Like who do ya mean?

BILLY: People I know.

DAGO: Everybody's gone mostly.

BILLY: Yeah?

DAGO: Except ya know who I saw?

BILLY: Who?

DAGO: Tommy Rifkin.

BILLY: Get out, Tommy Rifkin!?

DAGO: Yup.

BILLY: Whatever happened to him?

DAGO: He's colonial now.

BILLY: What?

DAGO: He's colonial. You know, like Ben Franklin.

BILLY: What are you talkin' about?

DAGO: I'm talkin' about Tommy Rifkin. "Under the tracks" Tommy Rifkin who used to get wasted with us.

BILLY: So what about him bein' colonial?

DAGO: I don't know. All I know is I'm walkin' down State Street and I'm not seein' anybody I know. And then Tommy pops outa nowhere and I see he's wearin' all that colonial shit... like stockings, and that triangle hat, and those stupid pilgrim shoes. I was sure it was him because I remembered his geeky walk.

DAGO: (Cont) So he's just ahead of me and I all the sudden remember he owes me fifty bucks he blew on the track a few years ago. So I go up to 'im and I go, "Hey Tommy." And I swear to God he turns to me and goes, "May I prithee help you sir?" Or somethin' like that.

BILLY: What is that?

DAGO: That's what I'm talkin' about. What is "prithee?"

BILLY: It's a colonial word.

DAGO: That's what I'm talkin' about. So he goes, "Prithee, may I help you, sir?" And I go, "Tommy, it's me, Dago." And then he looks at me like I'm nuts and so I just start askin' 'im what's goin' on with him. I ask 'im where he's livin' and he says, "I hold my estate in the great Commonwealth of Virginia, sir." And I go, "Oh yeah, where?" And he goes, "in the fair town of... Williamsburg."

BILLY: Williamsburg?

DAGO: Yeah.

BILLY: Holy shit.

DAGO: That's when it hit me too, that he turned into one of those weird colonial people at Williamsburg. It's like a cult down there... everybody acts like they're colonial and shit. That's why they call it "Colonial" Williamsburg.

BILLY: Yeah, but everybody acts like that just for tourists.

DAGO: No, I heard it. Some people go down there and they start wearin' those hats and those stupid shoes, and they just start bein' colonial and they can't stop. They're brainwashed.

BILLY: Tommy Rifkin is colonial?

DAGO: Yup. I mean what is that? Some guy you grow up with ends up being colonial. That's scary man. It's a cult down there.

BILLY: I guess.

DAGO: Nobody's who they are anymore Billy. Tommy's colonial, you're doin' this.

BILLY: I'm still who I am.

DAGO: Ya go away for a few years and everything's different. Everything's either different, or it's too much the same. It's a total crap shoot.

BILLY: Not everything's the same.

DAGO: Anyway, he tried to pay me back in that bullshit colonial money, but I told him to forget it. So, instead, I got two lifetime passes to Williamsburg if ya wanna go. He runs some kinda little red school house down there or somethin'. You know, like the "colonial schoolmaster" type thing.

BILLY: Wow.

DAGO: What do ya mean not everything's the same?

BILLY: What?

DAGO: "Not everything's the same." What did you mean by that?

BILLY: I just mean some things are different.

DAGO: Like what?

BILLY: Well like for one thing, I'm gettin' engaged.

DAGO: You're gettin' engaged?

BILLY: Yeah.

DAGO: To who?

BILLY: Gayle Maywalt.

DAGO: From our class, Gayle Maywalt?

BILLY: Yeah.

DAGO: Get out.

BILLY: What?

DAGO: Nothin'. I just can't see it. And how do ya know she'll say yes?

BILLY: I just know.

DAGO: Well then she's not right for ya.

BILLY: How do *you* know?

DAGO: Because, anybody you ask to marry ya, who ya know for sure is gonna say yes, is gonna say yes to anybody.

BILLY: What are you talkin' about?

DAGO: You're settling.

BILLY: How do you know?

DAGO: 'Cause I already know. You're askin' her 'cause ya know she's gonna say yes.

BILLY: Well who am I supposed to ask, somebody I know's gonna say no?

DAGO: No, somebody you think *might* say no.

BILLY: I like her. I like Gayle.

DAGO: Yeah, she's a nice girl. She'd marry me if I asked her.

BILLY: She looks a lot different now, Dago.

DAGO: All I'm sayin' is, be careful you're not takin' stuff just because you can. Make sure you want it.

BILLY: I know what I want. Look who's talkin'. When's the last time you were with somebody?

DAGO: (Wide smile) Last night as a matter of fact.

BILLY: Yeah, but when's the last time ya didn't have to pay for it? (Dago stops smiling and stares hard at Billy, who seems to regret saying what he did. He walks to Dago, but Dago turns away) Dago, I was only kiddin'.

DAGO: Yeah, everybody's a comedian.

(Billy turns from Dago, moves toward his desk)

BILLY: How 'bout it though? Haven't you ever thought of it... just hookin' up with somebody and settling down?

DAGO: What's the point? What's the point of bein' with somebody you're gonna end up makin' more sad then you already make yourself?

BILLY: Because, maybe it's better than nothin'.

DAGO: "Better than nothin'," is settling.

BILLY: "Better than nothin'" is better than nothin'.

DAGO: "Better than nothin'" *is* nothin'.

BILLY: Well than my "nothin'" is better than whatever you have.

DAGO: Hey, hey! Who am I talkin' to here? Billy you and me have to run as fast as we can, right now, from wherever we are, and end up wherever the fuck we end up.

BILLY: What are you talkin' about?

DAGO: I'm talkin' about just doin' somethin'.

BILLY: Like what?

DAGO: You ought to jump on a fast train, Billy.

BILLY: I told ya Dago, it's not like I don't want to.

DAGO: Look, my father said somethin' to me once. He said there's two ways to kill a goldfish.

BILLY: Kill a what?

DAGO: A goldfish. You know, the kind you win at a fair or somethin'.

BILLY: What about 'em?

DAGO: There's two ways to kill them. One way is to not feed 'em...

BILLY: Yeah?

DAGO: And the other way is, if the water in their tank is never changed, or if it's never touched, and it becomes too still, the fish start thinking there's something wrong, 'cause there's no motion around 'em, and they don't move. So they just stand there in the water real quiet and still, and then they just croak.

BILLY: Why?

DAGO: I think it's just outa sadness... that nothin' around them is movin', and I think after awhile they feel like what's the point of their movin' around when nothin' else in the tank is.

BILLY: Fish don't die outa sadness, Dago.

DAGO: Well think about it. People put those stupid little sculptures in the tank of divers or windmills or whatever, and they don't move. So the only thing that moves in a fish tank is a fish, and if it doesn't move, the water doesn't move... and if the water doesn't move, the fish will get depressed and then he'll just stand there and die... outa sadness. I'm tellin' ya, it's a well documented vicious cycle.

BILLY: That is so stupid.

DAGO: Think about it. Somebody puts a giant windmill next to you. The whole point of a windmill is for it to go around in the wind, right? If you were forced to live in a tank with a windmill that never moved... you'd die of sadness.

BILLY: Dago, shut up.

DAGO: I'm tellin' ya, the water in this stupid little office isn't movin'.

BILLY: Your dad told you this?

DAGO: No, I just said that. I always say my dad tells me things so people don't think he's a total lush. But it sounds like somethin' a dad might tell ya, doesn't it?

BILLY: I guess.

DAGO: Ya know what else my dad said?

BILLY: What?

DAGO: He said there's only one thing worse than being a sad fish dying in a still fish tank out of sadness.

BILLY: What's that?

DAGO: Being a sad fish in a still fish tank... and *not* dying out of sadness.

(Pause. Billy looks hard at Dago)

BILLY: Yeah well. Your dad talks too much.

DAGO: I guess. How 'bout it though? You ought to jump on a fast train, Billy.

BILLY: Dago, jumping on trains? I mean it's like the old west or somethin'.

DAGO: I came because I thought there was a chance you might want to come with me.

BILLY: Dago it's like askin' somebody to just drop everything.

DAGO: Every time each of us would do somethin'... the other one would too.

BILLY: But that was awhile ago.

DAGO: I'm not askin' ya because I thought you wouldn't.

BILLY: I'm just sayin'...

DAGO: Why not?

BILLY: It's not like I don't want to.

DAGO: Then just do.

BILLY: But I mean, Gayle...

DAGO: Everybody else I came to see is gone... or might as well be.

BILLY: *I'm* still here.

DAGO: So, then come.

BILLY: But...

DAGO: You oughta jump on a fast train, Billy. There's nothin' to it. It's all timing. You see it comin' and ya just watch it for awhile... and then ya start pickin' up its rhythm... because all trains, no matter how fast or slow, have a rhythm.

BILLY: I told ya, it's...

DAGO: Then ya get up close to it and ya see what kind it is, what kinda handle ya have to grab on to. Usually it's one 'a those small ladders right next to the doors, so ya start settin' your eyes on each ladder that's goin' by. And then ya tell yourself three more, and ya count 'em... one... two... *this* one! And ya grab onto it with your left hand and ya let the train fling ya out a little, so ya can feel your feet lift off the ground, like you're flyin'. And then ya swing back, just lettin' everything happen. That's where most people fuck up and kill themselves, when they try to pull too close to the train too soon. Ya gotta just let it do to ya what it wants, and then ya grab onto it for good.

(We start to hear the sound of a train, approaching)

BILLY: How fast is it goin'?

DAGO: The faster the better really. I hop on fast ones instead 'a slow ones 'cause on slow ones ya end up seein' the whole world go by, house by house, it's boring as shit. But on fast ones, everything's a blur, and the trees are just one big wall 'a green whippin' by, and best of all ya can't see anybody's sad friggin' faces. All ya can see is a quick flash of somethin' ya thought was somebody, but ya never know. It's a breeze goin' that fast. It's all timing and rhythm. I swear, when I'm next to a fast one I know I'm gonna jump on, my heart is beatin' just as fast as it's goin' by, and all I wanna do is get on it.

BILLY: You talk like this you make me wanna jump on too.

DAGO: All ya have to do is want to.

BILLY: It's not like...

DAGO: Just wait for the right one, Billy. Just keep your eyes on the ladders goin' by. See 'em? (The "train" gets louder)

BILLY: Yeah.

DAGO: (Seeing the train) Here it comes...

BILLY: Dago...

DAGO: Here it comes Billy... count 'em out!

BILLY: I'm not...

DAGO: Just keep your eyes on the ladders, Billy!

BILLY: Dago...

DAGO: Here it comes!

BILLY: Dago, it's...!

DAGO: Here it comes Billy. Three more! Count 'em out!

BILLY: Dago...

DAGO: One!

BILLY: Dago, it's not like...

DAGO: Two! Hook it with your hand Billy! Hook it!
  (The "train" is now incredibly loud)

BILLY: Dago...

DAGO: Hook it with your hand, Billy! Hook it! NOW! Shit!

BILLY: DAGO, I CAN'T! (The train sound passes us, starts to
  fade. Pause) I can't jump on any train. (Pause. Billy moves
  away, shaken up. Dago looks hard at Billy)

DAGO: Sorry, Billy.

BILLY: That's alright. Forget it. (Pause)

DAGO: I'll get outa here.

BILLY: You don't have to.

DAGO: No, I gotta.

BILLY: Where are you gonna go?

DAGO: Up north, I guess.

BILLY: Why don't ya stick around?

DAGO: What for?

BILLY: (Smiling) I don't know.

DAGO: (Extends his hand) See ya.

BILLY: Yeah. (They shake) Take care.
  (Dago walks toward the door, half exits, then turns to Billy and
  walks toward him with money in his hand)

DAGO: Here, just take the ten I owe ya.

BILLY: Dago...

DAGO: Dago Schultz is not a welcher.

BILLY: I told ya, if you don't pay me back, there's always the
  chance--

DAGO: --take it. (Dago puts the money in Billy's hand and
  stares hard at him. He then playfully hits Billy on the shoulder)
  Keep the water movin', Billy.

BILLY: I will, Dago. I will.

(Dago smiles and then quickly makes his way out. Billy stands still for a moment, then eventually makes his way back to his desk where he shuffles a few papers around. Then, slowly, he looks up and out the window. He is frozen as the lights slowly fade to black)

THE END

IT'S KINDA LIKE MATH

To Anne

"It's Kinda Like Math" was first produced in a workshop at The Yale School of Drama with the following cast:

John Papenberg, "Pap": Joshua Fardon
Jimmy Delfino: William Francis McGuire

The director was Jordan Corngold.

It was given its first professional production in Los Angeles at The Flight Theatre on a double bill with "Billy and Dago" with:

Pap: Shane Patrick McCullough
Jimmy: Peter Gregory

The director was Charles Evered.

The Characters

JOHN PAPENBERG, "PAP": Twenties, thirties

JIMMY DELFINO: Twenties, thirties

The Setting and Time

The play takes place in a room in the psychiatric wing of St. Mary's Hospital in Passaic, New Jersey. There's a single bed, with a couple chairs next to it.

The time is the present, visiting hours.

(As the lights come up and the music fades, we see Pap
sitting up in his hospital bed. We hear footsteps coming
from down the hall with a voice...)

JIMMY: Pap? (Pause) Hey, Pap? (Jimmy steps into the room.
He looks as if he's just come from work, flannel shirt, jeans
and work boots. In his hand is a visitor's pass and a folded
piece of paper) Hey, Pap. I wasn't sure where ya were.
How's it goin'? (Pap turns away a little) Ya weren't sleepin'
were ya? (No response) The visitor hours here are so stupid.
It's like they do everything they can to stop people from
seein' people. (Pause) Well... hey the room looks nice. It's
not like that sick green color in most hospitals. You know,
the kinda green they used to have in Lincoln School, remember? Miss Bartels tellin' us they were gonna paint the place,
everybody would get all excited, and then we'd see the
painters around and smell the paint, and we'd go out and see
it... and it wasn't a sick green anymore... it was a sick kind
of piss yellow, remember? (Jimmy inspects the walls) But this
is white. And white is nice, you know, real white. This is
real white. But that's not why I came Pap... I mean to tell
you that your walls were white.

(A long pause as Pap continues to face away. Jimmy suddenly
refers to the piece of paper he brought in)

Hey! I almost forgot. Everybody down at Apple Annie's
wanted me to give ya somethin'. We were thinkin' of gettin'
you a card, but it was too late, so we just folded up one of
these place mats and wrote on it. It has all those "how to
make a drink" recipes on it. Here ya go.

(Jimmy tries to hand it to him, but Pap ignores it. Jimmy
pulls it back)

JIMMY: (Cont) Well ya know everybody just said "hi" on it and everything. Nobody, you know... nobody thinks... everybody just thinks you're sick, Pap. Not, you know. I mean, whatever.

(Jimmy keeps the place mat in his hand)

So, has anybody else been by to see ya? (No response) I went by the old sporting goods and saw Mr. Davis. He still owns the place I guess. He was standin' by the bats as usual, and I told 'im you were doin' alright. He said to say "hi," so, "hi" from him. He was funny, because he kept on spurtin' out the same stories over and over again that he used to tell us when we cared. I mean, you know, about Vince Lombardi and Lou Gehrig and all that. He just kept goin' on and on about stuff and then all the sudden he just froze... and for a minute I thought he was gonna buy it, right there, because that big vein on his head kept pulsin' and I thought he was just gonna keel, but he didn't. He just turned to me and asked me all the sudden why we didn't come by as much anymore... I mean you and me, and I just told 'im, you know, it wasn't personal, but we had to work. The strange thing was, I don't think he saw me like I got any older. I mean he's pretty old now, but he looked at me like I was still a kid or somethin'. I don't know, I felt bad because I guess kids aren't listening to him as much now as we did then. So I just stood there and heard the Vince Lombardi story all over again even though I know I coulda told it right back to him, word for word. Anyway, he says "hi." (Pause) Well ya know what Pap, I'll just get outa here if you don't wanna...

(Jimmy exits, then immediately enters again)

JIMMY: (Cont) I just came by because I thought... I thought you might wanna talk or somethin'. But I guess since you're not talkin', I should take that as a sign you don't want to. But I can't, either, because I know sometimes when I don't wanna talk about somethin'...I clam up too. But the funny thing is, that's usually the time I want to talk about it most. I mean when I act like I don't, it's usually when I do, ya know?

(Pause, no reaction from Pap)

God, Pap... hospitals. I don't blame ya for not liking it here. There's somethin' about these places. The last time I was in one, was when I was little, and I remember bein' in and out all the time to see my sister, Amy, who was older than me then... I guess by about a year. And I guess still is older than me now... even though she's... you know.

(Jimmy seems a little uncomfortable, then continues)

Well, I'll tell ya one thing... I don't think I'll ever be able to go to Wallington Lanes again without laughin' or somethin'. I mean, in one way you could look at it kinda funny. "Pap freaked out... Pap freaked out!" I go "Whatdoya mean?" "He was in lane twenty seven and some body wanted to bowl in the next lane, and Pap just clocked 'im." "Why?" "Because Pap said somebody else was already there." "Who?" (Pause) "His Guardian Angel." (Pause. Jimmy laughs nervously) Well, it kinda shocked me at first. Then they told me you went around and wrecked the place... and that they put you in here. Just to kinda check you out and stuff.

(Jimmy turns, faces Pap directly)

JIMMY: (Cont) I didn't believe anybody at first, Pap. I figured somebody just picked a fight with ya or somethin'. But then I remembered you tellin' me all those stories when we were drunk... about how after your parents died you were so mad that you felt like you should get somethin' after somethin' was taken away from you... and how it's kinda like math, how if you're gonna keep somethin' for yourself, after some-thin's been taken away, then whatever's been taken away has to be replaced with somethin' else. And if God, or whoever wouldn't do it, then you had to do it for yourself. And so you joked around about how you rented a kind of guardian angel for yourself... and that he was there whenever anybody else wasn't. Well... I thought you were kiddin'! (Pause) But I guess when I heard what happened, it wasn't as weird to me as it was to everybody else. But it *was* weird. (Jimmy pauses, paces a little) But uh... I don't wanna bore ya, Pap. I guess I'm not tellin' ya anything ya don't already know.

(No reaction from Pap. Jimmy starts for the door, but makes an abrupt about face)

But ya know it's weird, because I only thought of Amy because she was here. Not this room... they have a floor for kids, I guess. I remember the room because it was the same kinda real white... but there was a window. Except I'm not sure why, because you couldn't see anything. They built some new something right up next to it. I don't know what she died of really. All I remember is her having tubes and stuff coming out of her, and my parents telling her not to play with them so much. I was only allowed up to see her like two times. Once when they brought her in, and then when they knew she was gonna... you know. I was supposed to leave right before, but my dad shoved me under the bed when the nurse came in, so I guess they forgot I was in there.

JIMMY: (Cont) It was real quiet in the room and I was falling
asleep on top of my dad who was sitting in one of the chairs
next to her. He and my mother could hardly stay awake,
because they didn't sleep for so long. And then real late I
guess, I remember somehow knowing that she was gonna die
right there in front of me. I mean right then, real quiet and
still, not moving or coughing or twistin' around. She was just
lying there... and every time she'd breathe she'd breathe a
little less. And once in awhile it looked like she was looking
at me... or I thought that... and she was telling me not to
wake up my parents. But she didn't actually say anything.
(He looks around) I guess the room was a little smaller. I just
remember sitting there frozen on my father... watchin' her
while she took her last breath, and I could hear something in
her stop, or kind of rattle, and the room was more quiet than
I ever heard it. And for a minute I felt like my heart stopped
too. Then what I'm talking about happened... with the window. This is the thing, Pap. This is what ya gotta hear if ya
haven't heard anything else I said. That I swear to God I saw
the curtains on the window fly up like there was a breeze
comin' through... but there couldn't be, because there wasn't
any room for it. There was a wall right next to it. And then I
looked at her again... and I know this is gonna sound crazy,
but I coulda swore... I coulda swore I saw an angel take her
out, Pap. Like... a guardian angel.

(Pap turns, faces Jimmy)

Now I'm not sayin' for sure I saw anything, and it might've
been in my head, but it didn't matter. See there's a place
between what's real and not, and this was one of those places.
And there was something in me that made me see her being
taken out a window by something I couldn't necessarily see
really. And I looked at the window again, and the curtain
went down. And I looked at her and she was still there, and
everything was quiet. Then the nurse came in and saw her

JIMMY: (Cont) and started screamin', wakin' up my parents. And then I remember somebody pulling me outside and I heard some kinda jolts, some kind of electric jolts or somethin'... and people running all over the place, and my mother crying and me just standing there in the middle of the hall, smiling, and thinkin' how stupid they all were. Because she was already gone. I saw her leave. I saw an angel take her out.

(Jimmy turns away from Pap, notices the walls again)

But white is white. Why do people make such a big deal about the different kinds of white? White's white. (He turns to Pap again) But just so ya know, Pap... I believe ya. Even if it isn't true. I believe ya. (Pause) And why not? Wallington Lanes, Wallington, New Jersey. On a Friday night my buddy John Papenberg went bowling. He had lane twenty seven and his guardian angel had lane twenty eight. And he got in a fist fight because somebody got outa line and tried to move in on the lane his angel was bowling in. And so now he's in St. Mary's restin' up. And that's that. (Pause) That's that.

(Jimmy and Pap stare hard at each other. Pap manages a little smile)

Well I'll tell ya what... I'm gonna get outa here before they start makin' up a bed for me.

(Jimmy moves toward the door, then realizes he still has the place mat in his hand. He moves to Pap and offers it to him. Pap takes it, as the lights fade slowly to black)

THE END

ONE CALL

To Tara McBride

"One Call" was first produced at The Renegade Theater Company, Hoboken, New Jersey with the following cast:

Danny: Doug Prochilo
Marianne: Katie Neuman

The director was Charles Rucker.

The Characters

DANNY: Late twenties, thirties

MARIANNE: Late twenties, thirties

The Setting and Time

The play takes place in a small visiting room in a police building in a small town outside a big city. There's a wooden table C, and a couple chairs next to it. Also, there's a sign that reads "No Smoking" hanging on the wall. There's a door L and another one UC.

The time is the present, three in the morning.

(As the lights come up we see Marianne enter from L. She's dressed in what appear to be her pajamas, covered by a raincoat. She enters tentatively, sitting at the table. Danny enters from UC. He's a rough looking but handsome man. He's wearing a shirt with blood stains on it, and a pair of ripped jeans. Also, we could see a small cut above one of his eyes. It's not till he moves down a little that we notice he's handcuffed)

DANNY: Hey, Marianne.

MARIANNE: Hi.

DANNY: This is kinda weird, I know.

MARIANNE: Well yeah. I mean I just don't get why you called me.

DANNY: I know it's been awhile.

MARIANNE: Well yeah, it has been. And...well...you know.

DANNY: Yeah.

MARIANNE: I mean...

DANNY: Yeah.

MARIANNE: I mean we don't really know each other.

DANNY: But you knew who I was when the guy called.

MARIANNE: Yeah. I mean I remembered your name.

DANNY: We went to high school together.

MARIANNE: I know. It's just that...that's all. That's the only way I know you.

DANNY: But you remembered me.

MARIANNE: Well. Yeah.

DANNY: Well, that's great.

MARIANNE: Yeah, I guess. So... what am I supposed to do?

DANNY: Well I don't know. I mean I've never been arrested before.

MARIANNE: Oh.

DANNY: Do you know who arrested me?

MARIANNE: Who?

DANNY: Frankie Giordano...from our class. Remember?

MARIANNE: Oh yeah. I heard he was a cop.

DANNY: I really never talked to 'im much in school. But, he seems like a really nice guy.

MARIANNE: Yeah?

DANNY: It's kinda strange...bein' back.

MARIANNE: Yeah, you don't live around here, right?

DANNY: No, I moved right after school.

MARIANNE: Where?

DANNY: All over really.

MARIANNE: I didn't see you at the reunion.

DANNY: Yeah I didn't go. How was it?

MARIANNE: It was alright.

DANNY: Good.

MARIANNE: So, the guy said you got in a fight.

DANNY: Yeah, I did.

MARIANNE: Are you alright?

DANNY: Oh yeah, I'm okay.

MARIANNE: Who with?

DANNY: Just some guy. It's stupid really. I feel kinda bad about it now.

MARIANNE: Oh. Well...you know. Uhm...so...why did you call me...don't you know anyone else in town?

DANNY: Well yeah, a couple people.

MARIANNE: I mean I don't really have any money.

DANNY: Oh no, I didn't call for that. I'll be alright. I just... I don't know... they just said I had one call, and it's been so long since I've been around... and... well I always wanted to call you... so...

MARIANNE: Well gosh, that is...really weird.

DANNY: Yeah I knew that...even when I was doin' it, but I did it anyway.

MARIANNE: And...no offense but...I don't remember even talking to you in high school.

DANNY: Well we didn't. We didn't talk at all. That's part of the reason I called now.

MARIANNE: Oh.

DANNY: I'm sorry if this is kinda awkward for ya.

MARIANNE: Oh no, that's alright. It's just kind of a surprise.

DANNY: It was nice of you to come down though. You didn't have to.

MARIANNE: Oh, that's okay. (Pause) So, how are things going for you?

DANNY: Well, other than being in jail, not bad actually.

MARIANNE: Yeah?

DANNY: It's hard to believe we've been outa school so long.

MARIANNE: Yeah it is.

DANNY: You look good.

MARIANNE: (Shrugging it off) Oh, that's alright.

DANNY: No you really do. I mean most girls pork out by now. But you look good...really.

MARIANNE: Thanks. You look good too.

DANNY: Thanks.

(Pause, awkward)

MARIANNE: So, where have you been all this time?

DANNY: Well, after school I went to college.

MARIANNE: Oh. Well, that's good.

DANNY: Yeah but...I didn't graduate or anything. I came up three and a half years short.

MARIANNE: What did you major in?

DANNY: Uhm...political...political...stuff...

MARIANNE: Political science?

DANNY: Yeah, pretty much.

MARIANNE: Well, that's great.

DANNY: It was okay.

MARIANNE: And then...

DANNY: And then, you know. My mom got real sick, so, I had to stay home with her.

MARIANNE: Oh, I'm sorry.

DANNY: That's okay.

MARIANNE: Is she...

DANNY: She didn't get better.

MARIANNE: Oh. (Realizing) I'm really sorry, Danny.

DANNY: Yeah, so then...you know, out there, lookin' for jobs...tryin' to find somethin' havin' to do with political anything.

MARIANNE: That's not easy.

DANNY: Yeah I know. I applied all over. You know, senators and all that. But that really wasn't what I had my mind set on.

MARIANNE: What was?

DANNY: Well, I know it sounds stupid, but I really wanted to work in the U.N. You know, The United Nations? I know it sounds stupid, but I really did want to.

MARIANNE: That doesn't sound stupid.

DANNY: Well, I called up, and this recording came on that tells ya to go there on a certain day and time, for an interview. So, I get all dressed up and everything, and I go down there, and I get on line with these other guys, and I all the sudden notice that I'm the only one on line with a suit on. Then this lady comes down and takes all of us into a room, and then they start askin' me questions, like if I ever had any experience in stuff like trash compacting and gardening and stuff like that.

MARIANNE: Oh.

DANNY: Yeah I felt kinda stupid, but I guess I shoulda' known. I mean I was sittin' there thinkin' they were gonna offer me a job where I could sit around one of those big tables and wear earphones and stuff like that.

MARIANNE: Oh yeah, those interpreter things.

DANNY: Yeah. God that was really stupid.

MARIANNE: No...

DANNY: How 'bout you?

MARIANNE: Oh, I just went to secretarial school.

DANNY: That's not "just" somethin', that's good.

MARIANNE: Well yeah. It was okay.

DANNY: Are you workin'?

MARIANNE: Yeah I've been with a place for a few years now.

DANNY: That's great.

MARIANNE: Well, I'm engaged, so, I figure I better start settling somewhere.

DANNY: Yeah.

MARIANNE: I went to college for awhile but...I don't know. I felt bad about being there ya know? Because I didn't really know what I wanted to do.

DANNY: "Live a happy life."

MARIANNE: What?

DANNY: "Live a happy life." That's what you wanted to do. That's what you said in our yearbook under "ambition."

MARIANNE: (Laughs) Oh, really?

DANNY: Are ya?

MARIANNE: What?

DANNY: Living a happy life?

MARIANNE: Well...sure. I guess. It's okay. You know.

DANNY: Yeah.

MARIANNE: What about you?

DANNY: What?

MARIANNE: What do you do now?

DANNY: Well. I'm in uh...liquor sales...mostly.

MARIANNE: Oh. Well...

DANNY: I mean I shouldn't say that. I mean I uh...I sell liquor.

MARIANNE: Oh.

DANNY: Well, just beer really. I sell just beer.

MARIANNE: Oh, like wholesale?

DANNY: Well no, not really. Actually...no, it's retail.

MARIANNE: Oh.

DANNY: I sell it retail at uhm...Shea Stadium.

MARIANNE: Oh. (Realizing) Oh.

DANNY: Do you know Shea Stadium?

MARIANNE: Sure, the Mets.

DANNY: Yeah well. I sell beer at Shea Stadium.

MARIANNE: Oh. Well...

DANNY: See I shoulda just come out and said that.

MARIANNE: That's okay.

DANNY: Actually that's kinda why I'm here now.

MARIANNE: What do ya mean?

DANNY: Do you remember Mike Delfino?

MARIANNE: Yeah, from our class.

DANNY: Yeah well, he's a businessman or somethin' now.

MARIANNE: Oh yeah I remember hearin' he's pretty loaded.

DANNY: Really?

MARIANNE: Yeah, like Fortune 500 loaded.

DANNY: Really? That is just so great for him. Anyway, he came to the game last night.

MARIANNE: At Shea?

DANNY: Yeah. And I was sellin', and I saw him there.

MARIANNE: Oh.

DANNY: Have you ever been to a game?

MARIANNE: Yeah, when I was little.

DANNY: Well at a game, when somebody wants a beer, and they see the beer guy walkin' around, they just call out for 'im. They'll say somethin' like, "Hey, Beer Man!"

MARIANNE: Oh.

DANNY: So I was workin', and I heard somebody up a few rows call "Beer Man," so I lug my rack up there, and I see it's Mike Delfino right away.

MARIANNE: Oh.

DANNY: So that's not bad really, except that after I said "hi" to 'im and told 'im who I was, he didn't even say "hi" back. He just kept callin' me "Beer Man," and laughin' real loud, and makin' fun of the stupid little paper hat I have to wear.

MARIANNE: What a jerk.

DANNY: Yeah, but it didn't even stop there. Then he started makin' fun of all the buttons I had on my smock. You know, the ones that say, "Lets go Mets" and "Welcome to Shea"...we are forced to wear 'em.

MARIANNE: God.

DANNY: Then he started askin' me if I had any connections with "Hot Dog Man" and "Ice Cream Man." That's when I started gettin' really pissed.

MARIANNE: Well, sure.

DANNY: Anyway, I...(Stops, refers to handcuffs) God I hate these things. I like to move my hands when I talk, and I can't now.

MARIANNE: Do they hurt?

DANNY: No, it's alright. Anyway, I really wanted to whale 'im right there, but I didn't. I kept thinkin' of that stupid saying about how there aren't any small jobs, just small people, and how if you're gonna be a janitor or somethin', you should be the best janitor there is.

MARIANNE: Well, that's true.

DANNY: Yeah it's true, but ya know what? It's bullshit. I mean fuck that. It still didn't make me not wanna kill 'im. So I stayed up all last night, just hearin' "Beer Man... Beer Man... Beer Man" over and over again in my head. And then today I took the bus over here, went to his parents house, asked them where he lived, went to his condo... that he owns, and I asked him to apologize and when he wouldn't, I kind of beat the crap out of 'im... right there.

MARIANNE: God.

DANNY: I know. It's pretty bad. But, it wasn't anything serious, and as you could see, he did an alright job defending himself.

MARIANNE: I see that.

DANNY: I mean I didn't feel good about it...even when I was doin' it. I kept hittin' 'im and apologizing at the same time. Bang!...sorry. Bang!...sorry.

MARIANNE: God.

DANNY: Yeah. Well, I'm not stupid. I mean I know my hittin' 'im wasn't just about him. It was somethin' bigger. I know that. (Pause, suddenly recalls) You're engaged!?

MARIANNE: Yeah.

DANNY: To who?

MARIANNE: Johnny Gahwyler.

DANNY: Do I know him?

MARIANNE: How do I know, I hardly know you!

DANNY: I mean is he from our class?

MARIANNE: He was two years ahead.

DANNY: Oh wait, big football Johnny?

MARIANNE: Yup. And track and tennis and...

DANNY: Yeah yeah yeah. You like him?

MARIANNE: We're engaged.

DANNY: God.

MARIANNE: What?

DANNY: I just never thought of you with him.

MARIANNE: What do ya mean?

DANNY: I mean it's just a surprise to me. And I'm sorry to say
    somewhat of a disappointment.

MARIANNE: What do ya mean!?

DANNY: I mean I always thought...

MARIANNE: What?

DANNY: Nothin'. I'm not sayin' I didn't like 'im. I'm just sayin'
    I always thought he was kind of a scumbag.

MARIANNE: Well he's not!

DANNY: Well maybe he's different now.

MARIANNE: He is!

DANNY: So you thought he was a scumbag too?

MARIANNE: I didn't say that.

DANNY: Did you like him back then?

MARIANNE: No.

DANNY: But you do now?

MARIANNE: We're engaged!

DANNY: So he's different now then he was then.

MARIANNE: Yeah, he's done a lot of growin' up.

DANNY: Are you sure he's not just an older scumbag now?

MARIANNE: I can't believe your sayin' this.

DANNY: I'm just thinkin' of you.

MARIANNE: Well who asked ya to?

DANNY: Alright, I'm sorry.

MARIANNE: And what do you mean you're surprised...like you thought of *me* before?

DANNY: Well...yeah. I mean you know...

MARIANNE: No.

DANNY: Well alright. I mean I thought of you with someone... but not someone like him.

MARIANNE: Who *did* you think of me with?

DANNY: I don't know. Who'd you think of *me* with?

MARIANNE: Who said I thought of you?

DANNY: Nobody. I'm just askin'. (Pause, Danny is dejected)

MARIANNE: Alright, I did. I did think of you.

DANNY: Who with?

MARIANNE: Nobody really. I never thought of you with anybody. I always kinda thought of you as alone.

DANNY: I was alone.

MARIANNE: Then I guess that's why I thought of you that way.

DANNY: (With a smile) But you did think of me.

MARIANNE: I said that already.

DANNY: Did you think of me as kinda cute?

MARIANNE: No.

DANNY: Not even in a kinda weird way?

MARIANNE: No, not really. I mean, no offense.

DANNY: Well I don't think you should marry this guy.

MARIANNE: I don't really think it's any of your business.

DANNY: Alright, alright.

MARIANNE: It's not like you have any right to judge anybody.

DANNY: What do ya mean?

MARIANNE: I mean you're not exactly in a position to pass judgement right now.

DANNY: How do ya know I'm not in the exact position I want to be in right now?

MARIANNE: Because you're all bloody...and you're in jail.

DANNY: *And* I'm talkin' to you.

MARIANNE: So?

DANNY: So?

MARIANNE: So what? You coulda talked to me anywhere.

DANNY: Not like this.

MARIANNE: Like what?

DANNY: The way we're talkin' right now. How do you know all this hasn't been totally calculated?

MARIANNE: Because that would be an incredibly stupid thing to do.

DANNY: Or an incredibly brilliant thing to do. I called you, and I haven't seen you in ten years.

MARIANNE: So?

DANNY: So, doesn't that make you think about anything?

MARIANNE: Yeah, it makes me think that you're very strange.

DANNY: And there ya go thinking about me again. You can't get me off outa your head. I'm telling ya, don't marry him. He's a bum. I called just in time.

MARIANNE: How could you call him a bum...looking the way you do...in handcuffs!

DANNY: I'm just...(He makes an attempt to raise his hands, but can't) Ouch!

MARIANNE: What's the matter?

DANNY: I can't stand talkin' like this. I wanna move my hands.

MARIANNE: Oh.

DANNY: Do you love this guy?

MARIANNE: I can not believe this!

DANNY: I'm just askin'!

MARIANNE: Yeah. I love him...okay.

DANNY: You love him...okay?

MARIANNE: Yeah. I...I...I...

DANNY: --love him okay.

MARIANNE: That's right.

DANNY: No offense, but I ain't buyin' it lady.

MARIANNE: Who are you to buy it or not?

DANNY: I remember the last party our class had together. I was standin' by Christine Belford's pool, and you came over to me,

DANNY: (Cont) and you said that you were sorry that we never talked, and that you thought you would've liked me very much.

MARIANNE: So?

DANNY: So...

MARIANNE: So those are the kinda things you say in high school.

DANNY: Well, I believed it!

MARIANNE: And so on that you base a phone call after ten plus years?

DANNY: That and other things.

MARIANNE: What other things?

DANNY: Amanda.

MARIANNE: Amanda who?

DANNY: Amanda your best friend from high school Amanda.

MARIANNE: What about her?

DANNY: I talked to her.

MARIANNE: So?

DANNY: She told me.

MARIANNE: What? (Pause)

DANNY: Are you gonna make me say it?

MARIANNE: What?

DANNY: She told me you thought I was cute..."in a kind of weird way"...and that you thought I had a nice...

MARIANNE: What?

DANNY: You know...

MARIANNE: What!

DANNY: (Gesturing with his head) You know!

MARIANNE: WHAT!

DANNY: BUTT! She said you said I had a nice butt.

MARIANNE: So?

DANNY: So you had a crush on me.

MARIANNE: Years ago!

DANNY: But all this is a far cry from what you said...and how you acted when I first came in here.

MARIANNE: I can't believe this.

DANNY: I'm telling ya Marianne, drop this guy. You've got a lot of growin' up to do. Do what I tell ya. He's not worth it. We don't have to see each other right away. I understand, you're gonna need some space.

MARIANNE: Oh my God.

DANNY: Do ya want my number?

MARIANNE: No.

DANNY: I'm not listed. You better take it.

(Marianne begins preparing to leave)

MARIANNE: I don't care.

(She opens the door partially, then stops)

DANNY: I really do think I called just in time.

MARIANNE: You're crazy.

DANNY: Whatever. Take my number.

MARIANNE: No...

DANNY: Call collect.

MARIANNE: I can't!

DANNY: 935-51...

MARIANNE: I'M ENGAGED! (Danny is taken aback. He turns away slowly toward the other end of the room. Marianne takes a half step out, then stops, turns to him) Danny I'm sorry. Believe me, I'm just flattered somebody's been thinking of me. And enough to waste their only call on me. Anyway, I hope everything works out for you. (Pause) See ya.

(She slowly walks out the door. Danny stands still for a moment. Then, suddenly, Marianne bursts back into the room with a pad and pencil in hand)

DANNY: 935-5109.

(Marianne quickly dashes the numbers down)

MARIANNE: I probably won't call.

DANNY: It only takes one. (Marianne smiles, then breezes out, shutting the door quickly behind her. Danny speaks to the closed door) See ya, Marianne. (Danny stands still again for a moment, then makes his way over to the door UC and kicks it hard several times) Hey! Let me outa here!

(He turns around again and faces the door where Marianne just exited. He walks over to it and smiles as the lights begin to fade and the music comes up)

THE END

RUNNING FUNNY

For Ree Ree

"Running Funny" was first produced at The Williamstown Theatre Festival's Studio Theatre with the following cast:

Michael: Paul Giamatti
Eddie: Nick Brooks
Stan: Peter Gregory

The director was Bonnie J. Monte.

The Characters

MICHAEL: Twenties

EDDIE: Twenties

STAN: Sixties. Blind

The Setting and Time

The play takes place in a garage in a small town outside a big city.
The space has been converted into a "kind of" apartment. There's
a door L, and a small hanging mirror next to it. There are several
old license plates and posters hanging on the walls. There are two
army cots UC, a small television on a table DC, assorted broken
lawn chairs, a lawn mower, garden tools, etc. The garage is lit by
a few hanging light bulbs.

The play is divided into ten scenes separated by brief intervals of
darkness and music.

The time is the present.

Scene One. May 30th

> (As the lights come up and the music fades, we see Eddie and Michael standing near the opened door. Having just entered, they are putting their bags down. Michael has a small suitcase, Eddie has a duffle bag)

MICHAEL: It's a garage.

EDDIE: It's an "apartment garage."

MICHAEL: It's a garage, Ed.

EDDIE: Not, really.

MICHAEL: It's separate from the house, though.

EDDIE: Apartments can be too.

MICHAEL: There's garden tools on the walls.

EDDIE: So?

MICHAEL: It's a garage, Ed!

EDDIE: It can be both! (Gestures toward television) What's that?

MICHAEL: That's a television.

EDDIE: So, how many garages you know have televisions in 'em?

MICHAEL: This one.

EDDIE: So, what if it is a garage? So what? What's the difference between a garage, really, and a regular apartment with a sliding door for a wall and garden tools and stuff like that in it?

MICHAEL: Well...

EDDIE: (Gesturing toward cots) --there's beds.

MICHAEL: They're cots.

EDDIE: (Pointing) Pictures.

MICHAEL: Posters.

EDDIE: (Gesturing) Furniture.

MICHAEL: Lawn chairs.

EDDIE: You're just bein' picky.

MICHAEL: It's a garage! (Walks around) He should let us stay for free, the guy. There's no bathroom.

EDDIE: So, you have to pinch a loaf...you go in the house. You have to drain the serpent, go in the yard.

MICHAEL: God. (Notices) There's no windows...or phone.

EDDIE: We have a phone put in.

MICHAEL: I don't know.

EDDIE: It's just for a month. In thirty days from now we'll be in condos somewhere in the city. We send our resumes out, bang!

MICHAEL: I don't know.

EDDIE: I don't want to live with my parents. Do you want to live with your sister?

MICHAEL: No.

EDDIE: This way we're just living with ourselves...like at school, except this is *real* life now.

MICHAEL: I guess.

EDDIE: (Hushed) And our landlord...he would be blind.

MICHAEL: What?

EDDIE: He's blind, the guy.

MICHAEL: But he's wearing regular glasses.

EDDIE: So, a lot of blind people do.

MICHAEL: Why?

EDDIE: Some people are blind but don't think they are. They remember what seeing is, so they think that what they're seeing now, or what they "think" they're seeing now, is just seeing in a different way.

MICHAEL: Oh.

EDDIE: Yeah, to them, even though they're not seeing anything really...they think they're just seeing less of what they saw before they couldn't see.

MICHAEL: No, shit.

EDDIE: So this guy thinks he could see...and he can...in a way, but he can't.

MICHAEL: Huh.

EDDIE: I can tell by the way he thinks he looks at things. And that baseball bat. It's not a bat, it's a cane.

MICHAEL: It's a bat.

EDDIE: But to him it's a cane.

MICHAEL: Wow.

EDDIE: My grandfather was blind and thought he could see. And we had to act like he could too. Even though we knew he couldn't.

MICHAEL: God, really?

EDDIE: Oh yeah, every day I had to go show Grampa how I looked before school. "Go show Grampa." "But Grampa can't see." "Go show 'em anyway." And he'd say the same thing every day; "There's a sharp, boy. There's a sharp, boy." "Go show 'em anyway?" What the hell was that?

MICHAEL: That's pretty weird.

EDDIE: He used to say he could see my Grandmother all the time, too. And she died in 1936.

MICHAEL: God.

EDDIE: He's dead now too. Fell down an elevator shaft.

MICHAEL: Oh my God, really?

EDDIE: Yup. It's okay, though. He was gettin' on our nerves anyway.

(We hear a few taps of a bat near the open door. Slowly we see the baseball bat, then Stan, a man in his 60's follow behind it, using the bat as a cane to find his way into the garage)

EDDIE: Hey.

STAN: You boys know yet?

EDDIE: We're thinkin' about it.

STAN: No parties. No girls. No pets.

MICHAEL: Can't I bring my cat?

STAN: Nope.

EDDIE: How much for the month?

STAN: Three hundred.

EDDIE: Three hundred? If we wanted to rent an apartment we would've rented one.

STAN: This is an apartment. It's an "apartment garage."

MICHAEL: Yeah we know, but three hundred?

EDDIE: We just got outa college.

MICHAEL: We'd never make it.

EDDIE: We just got outa college.

STAN: Alright, alright. Two seventy five. But if I need help out in the yard you boys help.

MICHAEL: Okay.

EDDIE: Wait, what kinda help?

STAN: Cuttin' the lawn.

EDDIE: I didn't go to college to cut grass.

STAN: Take it or leave it.

EDDIE: Okay, we're gonna go with it for a month.

STAN: (Extending hand) Cash.

(Mike and Eddie go into their respective bags and rummage through them. They both return with crumpled bills)

EDDIE: (To Michael) I only got a hundred twenty. I'll owe ya the rest.

(He hands his pile of bills to Michael, who counts it all and hands it to Stan)

STAN: I'll get a receipt.

MICHAEL: Thanks.

(Stan turns, taps his way out)

EDDIE: Shit!

MICHAEL: What?

EDDIE: We coulda given him friggin' monopoly money for all he knows!

MICHAEL: Well, it's ours anyway.

EDDIE: That's right. And I'm tellin' ya we're ahead of the game. It's easy to just sit somewhere and just wait for things to happen. But, this is when it happens for ya or it doesn't. And we have to always go forward. Remember what I said my dad said?

MICHAEL: I know, I know.

EDDIE: "Doin' nothin' in this world is as bad as doin' less than nothin', 'cause it's not gettin' you anywhere just as fast."
(Eddie smiles, satisfied)

MICHAEL: Yeah. You're dad's in the circus, isn't he?

EDDIE: (Smile fades) Kind of, yeah.

(The lights fade as the music comes up)

Scene Two. June 6th

(As the lights come up and the music fades, we see
Michael and Eddie sitting in two of the broken lawn
chairs. They're facing DS, watching the phone on top of
the television set)

EDDIE: How many resumes did you send out?

MICHAEL: How many did you?

EDDIE: I don't know. (Pause, then, under his breath) Three
hundred thirty four or somethin'.

MICHAEL: What!

EDDIE: That's normal!

MICHAEL: Holy crap.

EDDIE: How many did you?

MICHAEL: Less than that.

EDDIE: How less?

MICHAEL: Four.

EDDIE: Four!

MICHAEL: Yeah.

EDDIE: As in four *hundred* or one two three four?

MICHAEL: One two three four.

EDDIE: That's not good.

MICHAEL: Well how could you send out so many? What did you
do?

EDDIE: I sent them out to everywhere.

MICHAEL: For what kind of job?

EDDIE: Every kind. Assistant to this or that, entry level
anything, Junior whatever, Aid to him or her, Associate
Junior Executive's Assistant...this is what you have to do. Out
of three hundred something letters...I have to at least get three
calls.

MICHAEL: Wow.

EDDIE: And we have to be careful about when they do call.

MICHAEL: What do you mean?

EDDIE: It's important. (He jumps up and begins pacing) First of all we never answer it before four rings.

MICHAEL: Why not?

EDDIE: Because it makes us look anxious. You can pick it up in the middle of the fifth ring...that's okay. But don't let it go to seven, because they don't like to wait, and seven rings makes it look like we're layin' around or sleepin' or somethin'. So, four and a half...to five and a half...to six rings is the best.

MICHAEL: Okay.

EDDIE: And when you pick it up, just don't say hello. Say hello and then your name and then tell them it's you speaking. Like this. (He picks up the phone and speaks into it) Hello, Edward Formisano...speaking. (Hangs up) See?

MICHAEL: Yeah.

EDDIE: And if I pick up the phone and it's for you, or you pick it up and it's for me, we're gonna put it on hold.

MICHAEL: We don't have hold.

EDDIE: Oh, contraire. (Eddie goes into his duffle bag and removes a towel and Pez dispenser) Voila.

MICHAEL: What is that?

EDDIE: Our hold. Watch. (He goes to the phone) If they call, and I answer, and it's for you, I do this. (He picks up phone, speaks into it) Hello, Edward Formisano, speaking. Yes I think Mr. Kaminski is presently available. Hold please? Thank you. (To Michael) Now you take the Pez and you hold it up to the speaking part like this, and you click it. (He does) That makes it sound like you clicked 'em on hold. Then you take the towel and you wrap the whole thing up like this. (He wraps the mouth and earpiece in the towel) There. Now they can't hear anything. Now they're on hold.

MICHAEL: I don't think it'll sound like the real thing.

EDDIE: It will. I'm tellin' you this is what you have to do. And there's a kind of system when you're talkin' to them too. If they call and say they'd like to see you for an interview, say fine, but

EDDIE: (Cont) as soon as they say what day and time they want to see you, tell them the day is fine, but that you can't come that time.

MICHAEL: Why?

EDDIE: Because it makes it look like you're out there talkin' to people. So whatever time they want to see you, try to change it to a half hour before or after that time. Like this. You be them and give me a day and time.

MICHAEL: What do you mean?

EDDIE: Just say what they would.

MICHAEL: Okay, uhm..."We'd like to see you Tuesday at 9:30."

EDDIE: Okay. Then I would say, "Tuesday is fine, but could we possibly make it nine or ten?" (Pause)

MICHAEL: What if they say no?

EDDIE: They won't.

MICHAEL: But what if they do?

EDDIE: They're not gonna.

MICHAEL: But what if they do?

EDDIE: Then you say 9:30 is alright.

MICHAEL: But then they'll wonder why you wanted to change it.

EDDIE: So then you...you just...What are you talkin' about!? They're not gonna say no!

MICHAEL: Well it doesn't matter anyway, because nobody's callin'.

EDDIE: So that's normal. It takes time for the letters to get there. It takes time for them to open them. It takes time for them to read them. And then they call. Give it two more days.
(Eddie wanders slowly to the phone again, picks it up and checks for the dial tone. After hanging up he goes back to his chair. Michael then gets up gradually and wanders to a spot near the phone. He stops and stares at it as the music comes up and the lights fade to black)

Scene Three. June 8th

> (As the lights come up slowly and the music fades, Eddie
> and Michael are standing near the phone again. Eddie
> looks at the phone and breathes the word "Assholes"
> under his breath. The lights go to black as the music
> comes up)

Scene Four. June 11th

> (As the lights come up and the music fades, we see
> Michael holding the baseball bat and pacing the floor in
> front of Stan, who is seated on one of the broken lawn
> chairs. Michael starts as soon as the lights come up)

MICHAEL: Ted Williams was the greatest baseball player that
ever lived.

STAN: Oh yeah?

MICHAEL: Yup. Nobody knew more about what they were doin'
than he did. "Practice, practice, practice. Always take the first
pitch. Know your zone. Make them pitch to you. Hit through
the ball, not on top of it." I musta read his book like fifty times.
I don't think there was anybody in the whole world who knew
more about hitting a baseball.

STAN: Yeah?

MICHAEL: Yup. (Noticing bat) This is a real Louisville Slugger,
isn't it?

STAN: Yup.

MICHAEL: Where'd ya get it?

STAN: It's my boy's.

MICHAEL: Oh, he played?

STAN: Sure.

MICHAEL: How about you, Stan?

STAN: Oh, I played in the service. That's how I hurt my knee. (Rubs his knee) And boy does it hurt.

MICHAEL: In school did ya play?

STAN: No, we didn't play in school. After school we used to play what they called caddy...with a stick, and then another stick like this...(Demonstrates). We couldn't get any balls and bats back then. That was for rich kids.

MICHAEL: I used to play.

STAN: Oh, yeah?

MICHAEL: Yeah but...I stopped after I got to high school.

STAN: Why's that...ya get hurt?

MICHAEL: (Swinging the bat limply) No. I don't know. (Pause) I used to...I don't know.

STAN: What?

MICHAEL: I'm not sure but...I think I used to run funny or somethin'.

STAN: Run funny?

MICHAEL: Yeah, see I wasn't a power hitter or anything, so it wasn't like I hit a lot of homers. But I did hit one once. It wasn't a shot over the fence, because there wasn't one. It was one of those open fields, ya know?

STAN: Yeah.

MICHAEL: Anyway, this one time I hit a line drive to right center and it skidded between the guys out there and just kept goin' because they cut the grass short. So, I took off. And I remember knowing when I rounded second that I'd get a homer out of it...but I didn't hear anybody screamin' or goin' crazy for me. I just remember hearing...laughin'.

STAN: Laughin'?

MICHAEL: Yeah. It was like the canned stuff you hear on T.V. It was that clear.

STAN: No kiddin'.

MICHAEL: Yeah, and when I made it home...and I didn't even have to slide or anything, everybody was bent over...cracking up. I mean *everybody*...the catcher, and the umpire, and the whole rest of both teams. Everybody was red in the face goin'

MICHAEL: (Cont) nuts. I didn't know what happened, so I just kinda started laughin' too. Just to go along with it. Then Billy Brooks came up to me and told me I ran funny...like an ostrich.

STAN: You ran like an ostrich?

MICHAEL: Yeah, I guess. (Pause) I just laughed again and told him I knew, like I planned to make everybody laugh by running like an ostrich when I hit my first home run. But... I don't know. I just remember thinkin' to myself that if this is what happens when ya hit a home run... then to heck with it. So every time I got up after that I struck out on purpose just so I wouldn't have to run in front of anybody anymore.

STAN: That's too bad.

MICHAEL: Yeah. (Pause) I mean by then baseball was fadin' to me anyway. Everything was different. My mom and dad were gone so, it wasn't like it was. I didn't care anymore anyway because... I don't know.

STAN: Your mom and dad...

MICHAEL: --yeah my parents both died at the same time when I was a kid.

STAN: Oh. (Pause)

MICHAEL: You live alone Stan, right?

STAN: Yeah. My Rita's gone almost twenty years now.

MICHAEL: Wow. Do you see your son much or...

STAN: Oh yeah. He comes to visit me.

MICHAEL: That's good. (Pause) But...he's not around much?

STAN: Well he's in California. And California's a whole different ball game.

MICHAEL: Yeah, I guess. (Pause)

STAN: Did you boys get a job yet?

MICHAEL: Nope. No calls yet.

STAN: You're all done with school?

MICHAEL: Yeah.

STAN: Gonna make big money...with college.

MICHAEL: Yeah, sure.

STAN: My boy's got a big job with computers. He's always on a plane somewhere...and they give 'im his own car.

MICHAEL: Yeah?

STAN: Yup. He's a manager. Manages the offices. He brought one office up sixty...to sixty eight percent.

MICHAEL: Wow. (Pause) What does that mean?

STAN: I don't know, but it's good.

MICHAEL: Oh. (Pause)

STAN: So what are you gonna do with your life?

MICHAEL: I don't know.

STAN: You gotta do somethin'.

MICHAEL: Yeah I know. I don't know, one side of me wants to do that ya know?...get cars and stuff. But the other side wants to do somethin' else. Only I'm not sure it's anything even.

STAN: What do ya mean?

MICHAEL: I mean I feel like this is the time in my life when I can do two things really. I can do something. Or, I can do nothing. When I was in school, something was being done for me automatically. Now I either do or I don't...like Ed's dad says, but I'm not even sure what it is I'd do if I did, and what it is I wouldn't do if I didn't. (Pause) I mean a part of me thinks doing nothing is alright, but another part of me doesn't. It's hard when things inside you are going opposite ways, and you don't know which side to side with...because both sides are you. Ya know?

STAN: (Laughing a little) Yeah.

MICHAEL: What's so funny?

STAN: "Both sides are you." (Chuckles a little more)

MICHAEL: I know it sounds nuts, but it's like that.

STAN: Do ya have any pictures?

MICHAEL: What do ya mean?

STAN: Pictures.

MICHAEL: Of what?

STAN: Your folks.

MICHAEL: Uh...yeah. (Michael goes to his suitcase, opens it and removes three pictures. He moves back to Stan) Here. (Stan reaches out a hand and Michael places a picture in it) That's them before my sister. I think it's just after they got married.

STAN: (Holding picture up) Oh yeah, yeah. You look like your
    mother.

MICHAEL: Thanks. (Puts another in his hand) This is them at my
    sister's graduation.

STAN: (Holding picture backwards) Yeah, that's nice.

MICHAEL: (Gives Stan another) And this is them with me when
    I was thirteen.

STAN: (Holding it upside down) Oh, yeah. Good looking folks.

MICHAEL: Thanks.

(Michael takes the pictures, puts them back in the envelope,
    starts for the suitcase. As he's doing this, Eddie bursts in with
    a small brown bag)

EDDIE: Hey.

MICHAEL: Hey, Ed.

EDDIE: Any calls?

MICHAEL: Nope.

EDDIE: (Noticing Stan) What's up, Stan?

STAN: Hey.

EDDIE: (Removes a tie from the bag) Here it is. (It's a very wide
    tie, with a very loud and garish design on it) You like it?

MICHAEL: Wow.

EDDIE: Yeah?

MICHAEL: Well...

EDDIE: (Holding it in front of Stan) Stan, what do you think?
    (Eddie smirks) Huh Stan?
    (Pause)

STAN: I don't like it.

EDDIE: What?

STAN: I don't like it.

EDDIE: What do ya mean ya...

MICHAEL: I don't know either, Ed.

EDDIE: What is goin' on here? What do ya mean? This is nice!
    (Eddie holds the tie up, inspecting it again. The lights fade as
    the music comes up)

Scene Five. June 16th

(As the lights come up and the music fades, we find Eddie and Michael both pacing back and forth in the midst of a conversation)

EDDIE: College did exactly what it was supposed to do. It's your job to take the ball and run. You can't think of the time there as minus time. It was good.

MICHAEL: I'm not sayin' it wasn't good, I'm just sayin' I don't feel smart, really.

EDDIE: College isn't supposed to make you smart. It's supposed to prepare you for being able to act like you can handle yourself in situations you're not prepared for really. So you know how to talk about things just enough so people don't know you don't know what you're talkin' about.

MICHAEL: I don't understand that.

EDDIE: Well that's okay. You went to college. All you have to do is act like you understood that.

MICHAEL: I don't want to act like I understand things. I really want to.

EDDIE: Look, I'm just sayin' there's a certain way to be able to do things in life you can't really. Right?

MICHAEL: Yeah.

EDDIE: Now college gives you the license to act like you're able to do these things, until you move up the ladder and act like you can do different…more important things you can't.

MICHAEL: But I want to be able to do things I can't.

EDDIE: Well forget that. Just move up the ladder until ya can't anymore. Then, when you retire and you're almost dead, you can start caring about understanding things. But now it's stupid.

MICHAEL: I don't think it's stupid.

EDDIE: It *is* stupid, and you're stupid if you don't think it is.

MICHAEL: Then why is it that when I talk to someone like Stan, I don't feel as stupid as when I talked to people I used to talk to?

EDDIE: Because Stan is stupid.
MICHAEL: No he isn't. I think it's because Stan knows what he's
    talking about. And when I see he doesn't feel like he has to talk
    about big things, I don't feel like I have to either.
EDDIE: Why do you bother talking to him so much?
MICHAEL: 'Cause I like to. When I talk to Stan, I think maybe
    that's why I went to college.
EDDIE: What are you talkin' about?
MICHAEL: I mean I forgot that there's other kinds of talkin'. It
    just feels like for so long everything I've said's been directly
    related to what I read...like I've been puking words out of my
    mouth like a monkey for everybody to like me, and I'm just
    sayin' that I forgot what it was like to just talk to somebody for
    the sake of talkin'. Just to shoot the shit because that's what
    people do when they want to just talk to each other. Just to talk.
    And I'm sayin' college was good for me that way, because I
    care more about things, out of college, then I did when I was in.
    And I never would've known that if I never went in, so...
EDDIE: What the hell are you talkin' about? (The phone rings.
    They both freeze) HOLY SHIT!
MICHAEL: Get it!
EDDIE: No, you get it. If it's for me, put it on hold. (Ring)
MICHAEL: What if it's for me? (Ring)
EDDIE: They'll know it's you when you tell 'em! (Ring) Get it!
MICHAEL: Where's the Pez! (Searching frantically) Where's the
    towel? (Ring)
EDDIE: C'mon! (Searching) C'mon! (Ring. He sees the Pez
    dispenser on the floor) Here!
    (Ring)
MICHAEL: Where's the towel?
EDDIE: C'mon! (Ring) How many rings was that?
MICHAEL: I don't know. Where's the towel?
EDDIE: Oh, no! (Ring)
MICHAEL: It's not here!
EDDIE: Here! Here!
    (Eddie pulls his shirt off and hands it to Michael. Ring)

MICHAEL: Alright. (Michael picks up the phone, speaks) Hello.
   Michael Kaminski...speaking.

EDDIE: Good. (Michael gestures to Eddie to be quiet)

MICHAEL: Yes, Mr. Formisano is presently available. Could
   you hold please?

EDDIE: Good. Good.

MICHAEL: Thank you.
   (Michael holds the receiver up, clicks the Pez dispenser into it
   and wraps Eddie's shirt around it)

EDDIE: Good. (Michael puts the wrapped phone on the
   television) Alright I'll give it thirty seconds.

MICHAEL: Pick it up. It's only your mother.

EDDIE: What!

MICHAEL: Kidding. Pick it up!

EDDIE: Shh! (Eddie goes to phone, gently unwraps his shirt from
   around it. He then takes a deep breath, holds the phone up,
   clicks the Pez dispenser into it and speaks) Ed Formisano...
   speaking. Yes, yes... oh right... right... yes... Well, Friday
   is fine, but could we possibly make that two or three? (Pause)
   Oh. Okay. Well, two thirty is fine. Okay, right. Thanks for
   calling... righto now. Bye Bye. (He hangs up) Done. Friday,
   2:30.

MICHAEL: That's great.

EDDIE: The wheels are turning.

MICHAEL: That's great.
   (The phone rings again)

EDDIE: They are bangin' our doors down! (Ring) They're
   clamoring for us! (Ring)

MICHAEL: You get it this time!

EDDIE: Where's the Pez?!
   (Ring. Michael hands Eddie the Pez dispenser and his shirt)

MICHAEL: (Ring) GET IT!

EDDIE: One more ring. (Ring)

MICHAEL: GET IT!

EDDIE: Alright. (Eddie picks up the phone in mid-ring and speaks) Hello, Ed Formisano...speaking. Yes...yes Mr. Kaminski is presently in. Could you hold please? Thank you. (He's about to click the Pez dispenser, but then speaks into the phone again) Wait, this isn't the same guy that just called this number is it? Oh, Okay, good.

(He clicks the Pez dispenser into the mouthpiece and wraps the receiver up in his shirt)

EDDIE: This is it. This is our day. Now we're movin'. Things are happening.

MICHAEL: Give it to me.

(Eddie hands the wrapped receiver to Michael. Michael unwraps it and begins to lift the receiver to his ear)

EDDIE: Click it!

MICHAEL: What?

EDDIE: (Semi-whispering) Click it off hold!

MICHAEL: Oh, right. (Michael clicks the Pez dispenser into the phone, speaks) Hello?

EDDIE: No, your name!

MICHAEL: Yes, this is him. Oh right...yeah. Okay, bye.

(He hangs up)

EDDIE: What happened?

MICHAEL: Friday too. Me too.

EDDIE: What?

MICHAEL: Interview.

EDDIE: In the city?

MICHAEL: Yeah.

EDDIE: That's great!

MICHAEL: Yeah.

EDDIE: What time?

MICHAEL: Three.

EDDIE: Excellent!

MICHAEL: Yeah.

(Michael drifts slowly away from Eddie and the phone)

EDDIE: This is it, man.

MICHAEL: Yeah, I guess.

EDDIE: (Noticing Michael drifting) What's the matter with you? Do you realize what's goin' on here?

MICHAEL: Yeah.

EDDIE: What's the matter?

MICHAEL: (Softly) I miss my cat.

EDDIE: What?

MICHAEL: I was just thinkin'. I miss my cat.

EDDIE: You what?

(Lights fade to black as the music comes up)

Scene Six. June 20th

(As the lights come up and the music fades, we see Eddie sitting alone in the garage on one of the broken lawn chairs, watching a cartoon on T.V. He's dressed in a conservative grey striped suit with black polished shoes and a white shirt. He's also wearing his very loud tie. Michael enters. He's wearing a suit as well. It's an ill fitting brown pin striped suit. His shirt is wrinkled and the tie he's wearing is askew)

MICHAEL: (Upon entering) Hey.

EDDIE: Hey. (Michael walks to his cot and collapses in it. Eddie continues watching the cartoon for awhile, laughing at it, but then looks toward Michael who is lying face down in his cot) Well?

MICHAEL: What?

(Eddie jumps up, turns off the television)

EDDIE: What happened?

MICHAEL: (Sitting up in his cot) What happened with you?

EDDIE: You first.

MICHAEL: Did they say anything to you?

EDDIE: Like what?

MICHAEL: Did they say you got it?

EDDIE: Did they tell you you did?

MICHAEL: No.

EDDIE: Me either.

MICHAEL: So?

EDDIE: I think I did good.

MICHAEL: What happened?

EDDIE: Everything I thought would pretty much. I was pretty cool.

MICHAEL: Who did you talk to?

EDDIE: Some guy.

MICHAEL: What did he ask you?

EDDIE: Things about what I did.

MICHAEL: What did you tell 'im?

EDDIE: Whatever he wanted to hear. I just remembered the things like how to sit and shake his hand and stuff like that.

MICHAEL: What do ya mean?

EDDIE: I mean I presented myself good to 'im. And I did a little small talk and stuff like that. And I talked a little lower than usual, but I joked around a little too. And he laughed, so that was good. I think he liked me.

MICHAEL: That's good.

EDDIE: The office was nice though. And to get up to it, you have to go up to the security desk in front of the elevators and say your name. It's on the 56th floor the office. It takes like a minute to get up there, and they have special elevators for each set of floors. And when you get off, you see the whole floor is the office, and the windows are those long rectangle kind that window washers have to wash.

MICHAEL: Wow. So what did he say?

EDDIE: He said he'd let me know.

MICHAEL: So...

EDDIE: So, I don't know. (Pause)

MICHAEL: Did you wear that tie?

EDDIE: Yeah. He liked it.

MICHAEL: No way.

EDDIE: Seriously. He said it demonstrated my tendency toward creativity and individuality.

MICHAEL: Get out.

EDDIE: Yeah. I knew it would work. Everybody has a gimmick to show they're different from everybody else. So what about you?

MICHAEL: I don't know.

EDDIE: What do ya mean?

MICHAEL: I mean I went and...I don't know what happened.

EDDIE: What was it like?

MICHAEL: It was like yours I guess, but not as high up.

EDDIE: So, who'd ya talk to?

MICHAEL: Some guy.

EDDIE: Did you shake his hand?

MICHAEL: Yeah.

EDDIE: What was his name?

MICHAEL: I forget.

EDDIE: So, what did he ask you?

MICHAEL: About what I did and what I wanted and all that.

EDDIE: How did you sit?

MICHAEL: What do ya mean?

EDDIE: I mean did you cross your legs?

MICHAEL: I don't remember.

EDDIE: So, what did you tell 'im?

MICHAEL: Nothin'. He asked me what I wanted.

EDDIE: What do ya mean?

MICHAEL: I don't know. He asked me what I wanted from everything. In ten years or somethin'.

EDDIE: And what did you say?

MICHAEL: I told him I didn't know about ten years from now.

EDDIE: That's what you said?

MICHAEL: I told him I didn't understand what he meant. I told him I didn't know what to tell 'im. That whatever I did was on my resume, and I told him I didn't know what he wanted me to say, because I didn't like talkin' about myself. So I just sat there, and he looked at me with a pen in his mouth.

EDDIE: So...

MICHAEL: So that's what we did. I just sat there lookin' at
    him…lookin' at me, sayin' nothin'.
EDDIE: How long did this go on?
MICHAEL: Minutes.
EDDIE: Then what?
MICHAEL: Then he said he just wanted to connect a name with
    a face.
EDDIE: What does that mean?
MICHAEL: I don't know.
EDDIE: Then what?
MICHAEL: Then he thanked me for comin' in.
EDDIE: And then what?
MICHAEL: Then I got up.
EDDIE: Did he?
MICHAEL: No. He just sat there.
EDDIE: Then you shook his hand?
MICHAEL: Yeah. Then I walked out.
EDDIE: And that's it?
MICHAEL: Yeah. (Pause)
EDDIE: I don't know. (Pause)
MICHAEL: I don't know either. (Pause)
    (Lights fade as the music comes up)

Scene Seven. June 25th

>   (As the lights come up and the music fades, we see
>   Michael on his cot with a blanket on. Stan is sitting on a
>   lawn chair as Eddie does jumping jacks DL)

EDDIE: (As he's doing jumping jacks) The main difference
    between most people and people like me, is the difference
    between what we're doin'. Like me, right now, I'm doin'
    somethin'. (He shoots a look at Michael) As opposed to

EDDIE: (Cont) nothin' a lot of other people are doin' now.

STAN: (Confused, to Eddie) What?

EDDIE: (Growing more tired) I'm doin' somethin' now.

STAN: What are you doin'?

EDDIE: Jumping jacks.

STAN: Oh yeah? How many?

EDDIE: A few hundred.

STAN: Oh yeah?

EDDIE: Yeah. I used to do a lot more in school. I even got a Presidential Fitness Award for doin' 'em in fourth grade.

STAN: A Presidential award?

EDDIE: Yeah. (Red in the face)

MICHAEL: (From the cot) Everybody got those awards. (Michael rises slowly out of the cot, but the blanket remains wrapped around him)

EDDIE: What?

MICHAEL: Everybody got one.

EDDIE: (Huffing and puffing) Well, I got a special one.

MICHAEL: Freddy Maywalt got one, and he had asthma.

EDDIE: So he got one for breathin' into a tube good or somethin'. I don't know. (Eddie stops doing the jumping jacks and doubles over in pain, clutching his side)

MICHAEL: Are you alright?

EDDIE: Yeah. Pain means I did 'em good.

MICHAEL: I saw a box of a thousand of those awards in Mr. Matheson's office.

EDDIE: So?

MICHAEL: So there were only like a hundred kids in our school, Ed.

EDDIE: (Recovering slowly) And your point would be, Mike?

MICHAEL: It's just another somethin' that isn't anything when you look at it the way it really was.

EDDIE: (Collapsing on his back) Well, I'm just lookin' at it the way it really was for me. I don't care how many there were in the box. I got one because I did jumping jacks good. My mother

EDDIE: (Cont) tacked it on a piece of wood and immortalized it with polyurethane and she put it on the dining room wall. And it's still there. So I don't care what the heck it is. My mother thinks I got a special award from the President for somethin'. What am I gonna do...break her fuckin' heart? (Pause. He looks toward Stan) And what are you so quiet for, Stan?

STAN: 'Cause I'm not sayin' anything.

EDDIE: I'm gonna go run a few miles.

MICHAEL: No, you're not.

EDDIE: I'm not?

MICHAEL: Nope.

EDDIE: Well, what am I gonna do then?

MICHAEL: You're gonna run a few blocks, and then you're gonna get a cramp in your side, and then you're gonna start walking... and you're gonna say to yourself that walking's just as good as running really. It's really the same thing... only slower. So you're gonna walk to the Grand Union and you're gonna buy cupcakes and diet soda, and when you're guzzlin' that down your throat you're gonna say to yourself that it really doesn't matter what kind of food you eat, as long as you work it off somehow after you eat it. So, you're gonna walk... *walk* a few extra blocks, and you're gonna come back here and say you just ran a few miles, and you're gonna plop down on your cot and pass a lot of gas and watch Wheel of Fortune with me. So, the difference between you and me Ed, is that I'm just gonna lie here and wait until Wheel of Fortune comes on, and you're gonna put yourself through all that imaginary crap just to get to the same place you were already.

(Pause. Eddie and Michael stare directly at each other)

EDDIE: I'm gonna go run a few miles.

(Eddie jogs to the door, opens it, jogs out. Pause)

MICHAEL: Stan?

STAN: Yeah?

MICHAEL: Does this "apartment garage" feel like it's gettin' smaller to you?

STAN: I don't think so.

(After a few moments, Stan starts tapping his bat on the floor.
After he's tapped for awhile, annoying Michael...)
MICHAEL: Stan...
STAN: Yeah? (He stops tapping)
MICHAEL: Let me see the bat.
STAN: What for?
(Stan hands Michael the bat. Michael moves a little away from
Stan and lets the bat fall to his side, holding it with one hand.
Slowly he starts tapping it on the ground much like Stan did.
After a few taps...)
MICHAEL: I don't know what I'm doing. What am I doing?
STAN: I don't know.
MICHAEL: Look at me, I'm just standin' here.
STAN: Yeah.
MICHAEL: I don't know. (He taps the bat a few more times) You
ever really want to go back Stan...like back in time?
STAN: What do ya mean?
MICHAEL: I mean go back, but not like the time travel type of
going back. I mean just wishing and being back somewhere you
were...because it isn't the time you're in now...because the time
you're in now bites big time.
STAN: Yeah.
MICHAEL: Like the other night. I'd do anything to just do that.
I was at my sister's, and it was raining and windy and everything. And I just put on my jacket and walked out and started walking toward the house I used to live in with my parents. I just started walking toward it, making myself believe
my parents would be there ya know? Like all the time I lived
after they died was a dream or somethin'. (Pause) And then,
when I got near the house and I saw a light on in my mother's
old room, I made myself believe that she turned it on. And the
closer I got to the house, the faster I wanted to get there...until
I was running...and I was crying too because I knew it was all
make believe I made up inside my head, and I knew that any
minute I'd have to stop running and go back to where I really

MICHAEL: (Cont) was. And I didn't want to. (Pause, Michael looks away, as if toward someone else) "Yeah hi. I used to live here a long time ago with my parents...but...they're dead now, and I was thinkin' that as long as I ran here through the rain and everything...well I guess I just wanted to know really...if they were here..."

STAN: Mike?

MICHAEL: "See this real life thing, with all these tall buildings and everything...with all this go forwardness. I still don't know if it's all worth it really."

STAN: Mike?

MICHAEL: Yeah, Stan?

STAN: You okay?

MICHAEL: Yeah, I'm okay. (Pause) Here's your bat, Stan. (He hands the bat to Stan. Eventually Stan begins tapping it again on the floor as Michael stands frozen. The lights fade as the music comes up)

Scene Eight. June 27

(As the lights come up and the music fades, we see Eddie staring at the phone. Michael is lying on his cot with a blanket on, facing US. Eddie turns to him)

EDDIE: What are you wearin' a blanket for? It's summer. (No response) Three hundred thirty four resumes. One call. One interview. *Three* hundred! Do you know how much that cost me? Plus I had 'em printed on that nice avocado green paper ...plus matching envelopes...plus stamps. Jesus. (Pause) I just don't wanna be a circus clown like my father. I mean he's not even a real clown. He collects crap from all those big circuses, but he's only a clown at those little grammar school fairs. And my mother hates him being a clown too... especially when he drinks, and he sits at the table with his clown makeup on, burping and getting it all smeared in with all the food he's eatin'. God. (Pause) Man. (Pause) There is aluminum siding, though. My brother in law owns an aluminum siding business, and he said I could work for him if nothin' works out. (Pause. He looks toward Michael lying very still in his cot, then he wanders toward the small mirror hanging near the door. He speaks to his reflection) "Hi, I'm an aluminum siding salesman." (Pause. Another facial expression) "Hello, I sell aluminum bonded material to encase the exterior of domestic dwellings." (He gestures to his right) "This is my wife Inga, she's a Swedish model. And this is my son, Ed junior. He's a nuclear physicist, a Nobel Prize winner, and he plays for the Yankees on the weekends." (Pause) "And I'm an aluminum siding salesman." (Pause, still looking in mirror) Great. (Looking toward Michael) Mike? (No reply) Mike? (He moves toward Michael and notices Michael's cot shaking slightly) Mike? (He slowly retreats as he realizes Michael is crying) Sorry, Mike. Sorry.

(The lights fade to black as the music comes up)

Scene Nine. June 30th

> (As the lights come up and the music fades, we see Stan sitting in one of the broken lawn chairs, holding his baseball bat. Eddie is pacing the floor in front of Stan. Michael is lying on his cot, US)

EDDIE: The way I see it Stan, we're all on a train.
STAN: (Suddenly disoriented) We are!?
EDDIE: No, I mean like…what they call "figuratively," Stan.
STAN: Oh, okay.
EDDIE: Because I consider myself on a track…like on a train track…bound for somewhere. And if a train…no wait…see I took this "Great Ideas" class in school…

STAN: You took what?

EDDIE: I took a class in school called "Great Ideas," and I remember there was an idea in it that had to do with life being...or you being like a train, and life being the track.

STAN: Oh *I'm* a train.

EDDIE: No, everybody's a train, Stan.

STAN: Oh.

EDDIE: It's kind of like the idea with the arrow, and how if you shoot the arrow it doesn't really move, but it just goes...no wait it's not. Oh yeah it is. Okay, it's like if you shoot the arrow at somebody, it never really moves, but it just goes along an infinite number of points.

STAN: What do ya mean?

EDDIE: I mean anything...anything going somewhere isn't so much going somewhere...like where it's supposed to go...as much as it's just staying where it is...in different places...at different times.

STAN: What do ya mean?

EDDIE: I mean...I mean basically...this isn't what I wanted to get at. Just understand this Stan; when you're looking at something going somewhere, it's doing more than just what it looks like it's doing.

STAN: Okay.

EDDIE: And even something that isn't going somewhere...in space...in the overall picture, really is. Even though you can't tell. So, the rule of thumb in regards to things that move and don't move is, that whatever they're doing, they're probably pretty much doing exactly what they look like they're not. So, do ya know what I'm talkin' about now?

STAN: Not really.

EDDIE: So the train hasn't started yet, and I get on the train, and I sit in one of those seats facing opposite the way the train is gonna be moving. So, when the train goes forwards, I'm gonna go forwards and backwards with it...at the same time.

STAN: Yeah.

EDDIE: So, what I'm sayin' is…(Pause) Wait, I forgot. (Pause) Oh, okay! So what I'm sayin' is… Okay, I don't exactly remember the idea having to do with the train in that class, but I think my idea has more to do with what I'm thinkin' than the other one does.

STAN: Uh huh.

EDDIE: So I'm sittin' on the train. It's going forward, and I'm going backwards, and the train and me are getting to the same place at the same time…even though we're separate things goin' totally different directions.

STAN: Yeah but…

EDDIE: What?

STAN: But you could sit backwards in your seat.

EDDIE: What?

STAN: If you don't want to face the opposite way the train is goin', you could just turn around in your seat.

EDDIE: But you can't sit that way. Nobody else does.

STAN: So. *You* could.

EDDIE: But you can't. I would look stupid.

STAN: But you'd be facin' the right way.

EDDIE: Yeah, but that isn't the point.

STAN: Oh. (Pause) Well, what exactly *is* the point, Ed?

EDDIE: The point is… (Pause) Okay, the point…when I'm sittin' the way…when I sit in a seat facing the opposite way the train is goin', I don't see where I'm goin'.

STAN: Yeah.

EDDIE: I only see where I've been.

STAN: Yeah.

EDDIE: So that's not good.

STAN: No?

EDDIE: No, because you should see where you're goin'. Actually, you should see where you've been, where you are, *and* where you're goin'.

STAN: Yeah?

EDDIE: So...they should make all the seats in trains face the window straight on, so everybody could see where they've been, where they are, and, where they're goin', all at the same time.

STAN: Yeah?

EDDIE: But that isn't what I wanted to get at. That isn't what I was even thinkin' about. I don't know why I even got on that.

STAN: Oh.

EDDIE: *My* great idea has mostly to do with the idea that we're all trains, but some of us see, aren't even on a track.

STAN: Oh.

EDDIE: Like ya know how a lot of old diners are really old train cars that they made into diners?

STAN: Yeah.

EDDIE: Well, they only do that after the train car can't work anymore. Right?

STAN: Yeah.

EDDIE: I mean, I think. I'm not sure, but I don't think they build train cars to become diners on purpose. They're built for one thing, and then they become another...not by choice.

STAN: Yeah.

EDDIE: Well, my theory about trains is...that some of us who are trains...who aren't on a track...could become diners before our time, before we even get a chance to be a real train. And I'm scared of that. I'm scared of becoming a diner before my time, Stan.

STAN: Oh.

EDDIE: See how that's different from the other train theory?

STAN: I...guess.

EDDIE: And then there's the other kind of train. (He looks toward Michael) There's the kind of train that's on the track, and that's years away from becoming a diner... and that doesn't move at all.

STAN: What do ya mean?

EDDIE: I mean there's a newly polished shiny new train sitting on a track somewhere...with all the seats facing the right way,

EDDIE: (Cont) and the guy calls "all aboard!" and the whistle
blows, and the train goes nowhere. It doesn't move.

STAN: Why not?

EDDIE: I don't know.

STAN: But it really is movin', right?

EDDIE: No. It doesn't move. It stays in the station. See that's my
point.

STAN: But you said things are opposite of what they look like.
So, a train that looks like it's not movin'...really is. Right?

EDDIE: Well, yeah. In a big way I said that. You know, in space.
But really, it's not movin' at all.

STAN: Oh. (Pause)

EDDIE: I'm gonna do some pushups. (Eddie hurls himself on the
floor and begins doing very poor pushups. He counts the first
few out loud) One...two...threeee...(Now he's barely able to do
anymore as the phone rings) HEY!

STAN: What?

EDDIE: (Jumping up) This is it! (Ring) Mike!
(Mike lifts his head up from the cot)

MICHAEL: What? (Ring)

EDDIE: The phone!

MICHAEL: Get it!

EDDIE: I can't. (Ring)

MICHAEL: Just get it.

EDDIE: Stan! (Ring)

STAN: What!?

EDDIE: You get it!
(He grabs the phone and puts it on Stan's lap)

STAN: What do I say? (Ring)

EDDIE: Just pick it up and say it's this place...and that Mike and
Ed lives here! (Ring)

STAN: What?

EDDIE: GET IT!
(Stan picks up the phone)

STAN: (In phone) Mike and Ed lives here.

EDDIE: Who's it for?

STAN: It's for Mike.

(Mike stands up near his cot)

MICHAEL: Who is it, Stan?

STAN: (In phone) Who is it?

EDDIE: Get it, Mike!

STAN: It's Mr. Cooper, Mike. It's about the job you went for.

EDDIE: Holy...

MICHAEL: (To Stan) Ask him what he wants.

STAN: (In phone) What do you want?

EDDIE: (To Mike) What are you doin'? GET IT!

STAN: He wants to talk to you, Mike.

MICHAEL: Ask him what he wants to tell me.

EDDIE: What are you doin'?

STAN: (In phone) What do you want to tell him? (Pause, to Mike)
   He wants you to start Monday, Mike.

EDDIE: Holy shit... (Pause)

MICHAEL: Tell him...I don't want to Stan.

EDDIE: WHAT!?

STAN: (In phone) He don't want to.

EDDIE: What are you doing?

STAN: He wants to know why, Mike.

EDDIE: Me too!

MICHAEL: Tell him I don't like the way he looks at people.

STAN: (In phone) He don't like the way you look at people.

MICHAEL: And the way he makes 'em feel out of place...in a
   place they feel that way anyway.

STAN: Do I have to say all that, Mike?

MICHAEL: Would ya, Stan?

STAN: (In phone) He said he don't like the way you make people
   feel...(To Mike) What Mike?

MICHAEL: Out of place.

STAN: (In phone) Out of place...

MICHAEL: In a place.

STAN: (In phone) In a place.

MICHAEL: They feel that way anyway.

STAN: (In phone) They feel that way anyway.

MICHAEL: That's good, Stan.

STAN: (To Mike) I don't think he knows what you're talkin' about, Mike. Oh, he hung up.

MICHAEL: Tell 'im to piss off, Stan.

STAN: He hung up though, Mike.

EDDIE: Tell 'im *I'll* take the job!

STAN: He hung up.

MICHAEL: Tell 'im to piss off anyway, Stan.

STAN: He hung up though.

EDDIE: (To Mike) What are you doing?

MICHAEL: Tell 'im anyway, Stan.

STAN: (In phone) Piss off anyway!
   (He hangs up)

MICHAEL: Thanks, Stan.

STAN: Sure, Mike.

EDDIE: (To Mike) What are you doing?

MICHAEL: I don't know.

EDDIE: What?!

MICHAEL: I don't know. I just don't feel right with things.

EDDIE: What things?

MICHAEL: If I wanted to I know I could...but I don't know.

EDDIE: What are you talkin' about? The whole point of comin' here was to get somewhere else.

MICHAEL: I know. I just don't know.

EDDIE: All I know is, that you've been wearin' blankets...and you cry when I don't understand why, and you miss your cat.

MICHAEL: I do. I do miss my cat.

EDDIE: Okay, I admit. Giving ourselves thirty days was a bad thing. Things don't happen in thirty days.

MICHAEL: But somethin' did happen.

EDDIE: We could give ourselves thirty more.

MICHAEL: It wouldn't make any difference.

EDDIE: Then our time is up.

MICHAEL: No. Things are just different from what we thought.

EDDIE: The fuckin' grammar school white face drunk off his ass clown was right. If you don't do it when you can, you're not

EDDIE: (Cont) gonna. We're as much nowhere now as we were
    before. If you let it happen to you it'll happen, and it did. You
    gotta keep moving!
MICHAEL: I know, but I can't. I just can't move like you, Ed.
EDDIE: Well just do!
MICHAEL: But there's too much stuff in my head!
EDDIE: Then get it out. Stop thinking so much. I did!
MICHAEL: But I can't, like you.
EDDIE: Then why can I?! I don't understand how we can get
    along in what we thought was real life, and then when *real* real
    life comes along, everything is different.
MICHAEL: I don't know either.
EDDIE: In every school we went to I thought I knew you. Now
    I don't feel like I know you anymore.
MICHAEL: You know me.
EDDIE: Not like I used to.
MICHAEL: Me either, Ed. That's how I feel about me, too.
    That's why I'm sayin' somethin' did happen in thirty days.
    (Pause)
STAN: So, you boys gonna be stayin' another month?
    (Michael and Eddie both look at Stan, then at each other. The
    lights fade to black as the music comes up)

Scene Ten. Months later

> (As the music fades, the lights come up on Michael, who
> is standing in a pool of light. A blanket hangs over his
> shoulders as he speaks in the direction of the audience)

MICHAEL: Dear Ed, I wanted to send you this letter because I
    was wondering how everything was going with you. I know it's
    been awhile, but Stan and me were thinkin' about ya, and
    wondering where ya were, and what you were doing. So, I sent
    this to your parents house figuring you'd get it somehow.

MICHAEL: (Cont) Everything's pretty much the same here. Stan got me a job through a friend of his, landscaping and stuff, enough to pay the rent and keep alive anyway. I just cut the grass out in front here so it wouldn't die when the frost and all that came around.

(Lights down on Michael and up on Eddie, who is standing DR, facing the audience as well. He's dressed in his grey suit, with his colorful tie and a "My name is" sticker on his lapel)

EDDIE: Dear Mike, I finally got your letter. I've been on the road the last couple of weeks. It was good to hear from ya, and to hear you're doin' alright.

(Lights down on Eddie, up on Michael)

MICHAEL: I really can't say I've been doin' much. My sister and her boyfriend came by the other week. He's majoring in psychology or somethin' at college, and he started asking me all these questions about what I was doin' here, and whether or not I "came to terms" with my living in a garage. I told him it was an apartment garage, but he just went on sayin' how important it was that I realize where I was. He just wouldn't get off it 'till I said it. "Yeah , yeah okay," I said. "I live in a garage." Then he asked me what sorta program I set for myself...like for life. I didn't know what he was talkin' about at first, then I thought about it and said, "Yeah, I set a program for myself for life; the delayed entry program." Well, he thought that was kinda funny at first, but my sister didn't. She started crying and saying how ashamed she was of me and all that. Then they finally left.

(Lights down on Michael, up on Eddie)

EDDIE: My parents built me a separate entrance to my room, so I can go in and out without ever seeing them for months. And my mother put one of those doggie doors at the bottom of my door so she could just shove food under there without us ever getting near each other. So, things are pretty good at home.

(Lights down on Eddie, up on Michael)

MICHAEL: Me and Stan were wondering if you were up in one
of those high rise offices with those rectangle windows and
secretaries and all that.

(Lights down on Michael, up on Eddie)

EDDIE: I hope you're not still wearing that stupid blanket all the
time. I told my mother about it and she said you probably
thought you were Jesus Christ or somethin'. I told her to just
shut up and shove my food in. Anyway, I hope you are getting
out more. I was kinda worried about ya for awhile there.
(Pause) You gotta keep movin', Mike.

(Lights up on Michael. Both Michael and Eddie are in the light,
facing the audience)

MICHAEL: I think you were right Ed, about people being
different kinds of trains.

EDDIE: You can't be afraid.

MICHAEL: I'm not sure, but I think I used to run funny or
somethin'.

EDDIE: You have to always go forward.

MICHAEL: If this is what happens when ya hit a home run...then
to heck with it. So every time I got up after that I struck out on
purpose just so I wouldn't have to run in front of anybody
anymore.

EDDIE: "Doin' nothin' in this world is as bad as doin' less than
nothin'... cause it's not getting you anywhere just as fast."

MICHAEL: I just can't move like you, Ed. I never could.

(Lights fade slowly on Michael but remain on Eddie. We now
see that next to Eddie is a large black salesman's valise, with
the following printed on the side; Duraside Aluminum Siding
Corp. "Side with Us.")

EDDIE: Real to touch wood like finishes, brick like patterns, and a veritable symphony of styles with which to choose from. So, "when you decide to side, side with Duraside. We're the side to... We're the side to side to... We're the..." Oh, crap, ya know what, just buy the damn siding, will ya?

(Lights to black immediately as the music comes up)

THE END

PAPER KLIPS

A Collection of Short Plays and Monologues

The Short Plays and Monologues

Love Sync
Spinning
Our Boy
Clari and Suzanne
The King (Who didn't want to sell aluminum siding) and I
Kirby's Law
Jimmy Has a Tendency
Little Things
21st Century Fox

To Kevin O'Sullivan

"Paper Klips" was first produced at The Raft Theatre in New York City with the following ensemble:

Frank Favata
Jeannie Hill
Madeline Mancini
Robert Nissen
Damian Young

The director was Charles Evered.

"Jimmy Has A Tendancy" and "21st Century Fox" were first staged by The Othersyde Theatre Company at The Williams Center for the Performing Arts, Rutherford, New Jersey. "Jimmy" was subsequently produced at The Williamstown Theatre Festival's Studio Theatre.

LOVE SYNC

The Characters

DAVIE: Twenties, thirties

KEMP: Twenties, thirties

LINDA: Twenties, thirties

MARCIE: Twenties, thirties

The Setting and Time

A work site and a plush LA apartment.

The time is the present.

(As the lights come up and the music fades, we see
Kemp and Davie, both carpenters, at a work site. Davie
works as Kemp leafs through a Playboy)

KEMP: It's stupid that you're not goin', Davie.

DAVIE: I got jobs lined up.

KEMP: Everything you got lined up is half a days work. You
could go if you wanted to.

DAVIE: I'm not goin'. And ya know what? I really don't want
to talk about it anymore.

(Lights fade on men, up on Marcie and Linda in apartment.
Linda nurses a drink as Marcie leafs through a Playgirl)

MARCIE: I really sense some kind of underlying hostility here,
Linda. I suggest you go to this thing.

LINDA: I'm not going.

MARCIE: So go drunk. Take pills. Nobody's saying you have
to go to it conscious.

LINDA: Please don't talk, Marcie. And that magazine is
disgusting. I wish you wouldn't bring it in this house.

MARCIE: It's healthy, Linda. It's healthy to pretend. Now
when I go to bed with my husband, I have faces and bodies
etched in my imagination that I can pretend with. Which is
more than *you* have I might add.

LINDA: Shut up, Marcie.

(Lights up on guys, down on women. Davie is hammering)

KEMP: Davie, look. (Davie keeps hammering) Davie!
(He finally stops)

DAVIE: What?

KEMP: This hesitation and neurosis of yours wouldn't have
anything to do with a certain young lady, would it?

DAVIE: What are you talking about?

KEMP: What I'm talking about is that you're not going to this reunion thing because *she* might be there.

DAVIE: Who?

KEMP: "Who."

DAVIE: Who?

KEMP: Who do you think?

DAVIE: Who do *you* think?

KEMP: Who we're talking about.

DAVIE: Who *are* we talking about?

KEMP: Her!

DAVIE: Who's her!?

KEMP: Linda!

(Davie glares at Kemp. Lights down on guys, up on women)

MARCIE: You're not going because you're divorced.

LINDA: That's not why I'm not going.

MARCIE: Then I know exactly why you're not going.

LINDA: Why?

MARCIE: Because you don't want to see him.

LINDA: Who's him?

MARCIE: You know who.

LINDA: *I* know who?

MARCIE: Yes you do.

LINDA: Who?

MARCIE: *Him.*

LINDA: How do *you* know him?

MARCIE: Who?

LINDA: Davie.

MARCIE: So that's his name.

(Marcie smiles, pleased. Linda's pissed as the lights fade on them, up on guys)

DAVIE: She's married, alright? I'm happy for her and that's that.

KEMP: (Under his breath) Not what I heard.

DAVIE: What did you say?

KEMP: I heard different.

DAVIE: What kind of different?

KEMP: I heard she got divorced.

DAVIE: Well then I'm sorry to hear that. I hope she's doing alright... and that's all. (As Kemp turns away, Davie makes an ecstatic gesture as if he scored a goal in soccer. Kemp turns to him as he tries to disguise his euphoria) Pass me a beer, will ya?

KEMP: Sure.

(Lights come up on the women, remain up on both sides now. Linda and Davie both move C with their respective drinks. They face each other directly)

LINDA: Look at me. He probably thinks I'm some rich bitch who married for the money.

MARCIE: Well, aren't you?

DAVIE: Even if I did go, what would I say to her? She got outa this town and I didn't. And I was always the one talkin' about it. We were together great though... and I don't know, we dreamed a lot together like kids do I guess. You know, before Mr. Reality reared his ugly head.

LINDA: He thought he was so smooth back then.

DAVIE: I was pretty smooth back then, though.

LINDA: He thought he was Brando. Seriously.

DAVIE: Actually a lot of people said I reminded them of a young Brando. I used to wear this really cool leather jacket.

LINDA: He used to wear this imitation leather jacket. I never told him I knew it wasn't real leather. I think it would've broken his heart.

DAVIE: Her father really dug me though. He really thought I had balls for such a young guy. Like I protected her or something.

LINDA: My father could not stand him. He made me carry a steak knife in my purse whenever I went out with him.

KEMP	MARCIE
So what happened?	So what happened?

DAVIE: She just kinda took off on me.

LINDA: My father wouldn't let me see him anymore.

DAVIE: I kept calling and calling.

LINDA: He wouldn't even let me call him back.

DAVIE: Then I went down to her house and her parents told me she took off early for college. I couldn't believe she would do that to me. I never went near there again.

LINDA: When I got to college I made myself forget him, but I guess I didn't really. Then I met you know who... and the rest is litigation.

(Davie and Linda both move DC together, face the audience)

DAVIE	LINDA
Let's face it. We don't have anything in common anymore anyway.	Who are we kidding? We don't have anything in common anymore, anyway.

(They both take swigs, wipe their mouths in the same exact way and move US)

MARCIE: So you're not going?

KEMP: So, no go?

LINDA: Well I need to get away anyway. Might as well catch up with a few people.

DAVIE: I guess that chicken at The Holiday Inn isn't half bad, so, you know...

(Kemp and Marcie smile, picking up their respective magazines. Davie and Linda turn, face each other again as the lights fade and the music comes up)

THE END

SPINNING

The Characters

A man or woman, any age

The Setting and Time

To the audience.

The time is the present.

The first thing I want to say is that whatever I say that might sound stupid at first, isn't really. It's just that I think better than I talk, and it kinda takes me awhile to get across what I really want to say. But at the same time, I know when I end up saying it... it's gonna sound pretty stupid. So, any time I say something stupid, you know I knew it was gonna sound stupid, but I just didn't have much of a choice in the matter.

So, here goes. Okay, it's a short story. I'm not really religious or anything unless I think I'm gonna die soon. And I don't really go in much for spiritual "occurrences," but I think I kinda had one awhile ago. See, that sounded stupid. I know that. But believe me, when I thought it, it sounded smart. It's just that when I said it, it became a whole different story. Okay, so anyway, the point is, someone I used to live with isn't living with me anymore... because they're dead. See? Stupid. So, I've been kinda having a tough time lately, you know, not so much getting used to the idea that they're dead, but getting used to them not being alive. So, like a lot of people who just had a person close to them die, I went to a place I used to go with this person all the time. Only I didn't really go there "a lot" with this person... actually, we only went there like once. But, sometimes I exaggerate things to make them seem less like my actual life, and more like a movie I'd like to make about my life... if I could.

See this all has to do with this thing that I did. See, I went to this park where I went with this person only once... in my actual life, but several times in my movie life, and I stood under a clump of trees where we sat, and I started spinning around and trying to hum that kind of tacky "going back in time" music they play whenever somebody in a movie starts spinning around and going back in time.

See... I know this all sounds stupid. I know that. And I knew it before I said it, but I said it anyway, because it was the closest I could get to telling you what I was thinking. If I didn't have to tell you, and you just knew what I wanted to say, it would sound much smarter. It's just because I'm forced to say it that it sounds stupid.

Okay, so I'm spinning around like this for awhile and I end up spinning myself right into one of the trees. Straight on. Bang. Well, I knew first of all that what happened actually did happen, because I was bleeding from my nose pretty bad. I mean I was visiting a place I had been to only once before... in my actual life, and I was spinning around trying to make myself go back in time so I could be with this person again.

Well, it's at this point where I'm kinda tempted to say that this person's ghost or something came back and told me to get over their not being there anymore... but it didn't. Nothing like that happened. Although later, if you're disapointed with the truth like I usually am, I can tell you that happened in a convincing enough way to make you think it actually did. But for now, I'm just gonna sum it up as quick and as un-stupid as possible.

Okay, so I'm lying in the grass bleeding from my nose and it kind of dawned on me that this person wasn't ever going to come back, and that I better stop bashing myself into trees because I could really hurt myself that way. (Pause) Well yeah, that's it. I mean the point is, I guess, that some people have to put themselves through different kinds of things to get them through things. And that's what I put myself through.

Okay, I sounded stupid again, but don't say I didn't warn you.

OUR BOY

The Characters

THE BOY: A man in his thirties or forties

JOYCE: Sixties, seventies

FRANK: Sixties, seventies

The Setting and Time

Joyce and Frank's suburban home.

The time is the present.

(As the lights come up and the music fades, we see the boy lying face down, near the couch, dressed in a conservative three piece suit. He remains there, perfectly still, throughout. Frank and Joyce are seated on two chairs)

JOYCE: Oh, don't worry. He's not dead. He's our boy. He's close to the ground, as usual. He's always liked to be close to the ground. The closer to the ground the better as far as he's concerned.

FRANK: Yup. That's our boy.

JOYCE: To have a son so close to the ground like that. Like an ethnic person's car.

FRANK: Yup.

JOYCE: He's a lawyer. He's got several degrees. At one school, he wouldn't even go up to the podium to get his diploma.

FRANK: Three steps. Three too many.

JOYCE: Nope. Didn't even go up to the podium.

FRANK: They had to throw it down to 'im.

JOYCE: Closer to the ground that way. He's a lawyer, our boy. Went to school to be a lawyer.

FRANK: Only law school in the country with only one floor.

JOYCE: He's never even been on an elevator.

FRANK: Can you imagine, having a son that stays like that, close to the ground?

JOYCE: And if he can't lie on the floor, he's always got to have a hand or a foot on it.

FRANK: He usually stays in the basement. He gets like this whenever we ask him to come up.

JOYCE: He crawled until he was twenty three years old. That's when he stopped wetting the mattress. Mind you he'd never sleep on a bed. It's not close enough to the ground for him.

FRANK: Got married... wouldn't even have any children. I'm
ashamed to say why. I can hardly say it, mother. Help me
Jesus, I can hardly say it.

JOYCE: He wouldn't get on top of her. He wouldn't get on top
of her because then she would be closer to the ground than he
was. And he wouldn't do it any other way. So, he gets a
divorce and he comes back home and he lies on the floor like
this. All day long.

FRANK: There was always somethin' about him.

JOYCE: We thought it was just a phase.

FRANK: Sent him to the best doctors. But he wouldn't go up to
see 'em.

JOYCE: Hospitals always have so many floors.

FRANK: They examined him on the hospital lawn, behind
some bushes.

JOYCE: Couldn't find a thing.

FRANK: Couldn't find a God Damn thing. Ruined our lives.

JOYCE: We can't have parties or friends over with our son
lying on the floor like that.

FRANK: We had one party.

JOYCE: Oh, we had some people over once. They were polite
and they didn't say anything. But I know they were thinking
things, because he was lying in the middle of the floor... like
that. We made him a little drink, and he drank it there on the
ground with a straw while people stepped over him.

FRANK: But he can't last. He's gotta die soon. Nobody can
live like that. What kind of a life is that?

JOYCE: Truth be told, he prefers first floors to basements,
since first floors are actually more level with the ground. The
reason he stays in the basement most of the time is because
it's close to the ground and more private. There's always
someone on the first floor, while there's usually no one in the
basement. So, as I said, given the choice, he would prefer to
be in the basement alone than on the first floor with someone
else. Actually, he'd prefer to be on the first floor alone, but
we can't live around him. We can't let him run our lives.

FRANK: The kitchen is on the first floor.

JOYCE: We have to eat.

FRANK: No one can live like this.

JOYCE: What am I supposed to do? I'm his mother. I can't throw him out just because he's always liked to be close to the ground.

FRANK: What could we do?

JOYCE: He's our boy.

(The music comes up as the lights fade slowly to black)

THE END

CLARI AND SUZANNE

The Characters

A WOMAN: Early twenties

The Setting and Time

To the audience.

The time is the present.

Okay, I was like goin' to school at avsha, or A.V.S.H.A., which if you live in my town really means somethin', because until it burnt down, it was like totally one of the best schools you could go to. Avsha stands for Anthony Vespuciato's School of Hair Artistry, and it was really a great place to go, except that we had to wear this like really geeky white uniform that made us look like we worked in a bakery or somethin'. The school was run by Tony... nobody really calls him Anthony, and he was a really cool guy... except that I think he burnt the place down on purpose because he was pissed off at Ida, his seventh wife, but that is a whole 'nother story. Anyway, the worst thing about the place burning down was that a lot of us lost our mannequin heads that we used to practice on, because when you do what I do, your mannequin head is essential. Some of us even started naming our mannequin heads and stuff, just as a kind of goof. I named mine Suzanne, after my best friend Suzanne, who ended up going with my *ex*-best friend Ron, but that is a whole 'nother story. Anyway, the thing is, my other friend Marcie was goin' there too, to avsha, and we were pretty good friends and everything, until... the fire.

See the first day of class, we all get our mannequin heads and mannequin head cases to carry them in or we'd look pretty geeky walkin' around with heads on our shoulders. I mean, da. It's geeky enough to have to carry them at all. So anyway, me and Marcie were gettin' along and everything until we go to school this one day... and we notice that like... the whole building is like... burning down? So Marcie and me just start screaming because we both left our heads there overnight. And Marcie is really like, freaking, because she was like really close to her mannequin head, Clari, who she named after her ex-best friend Clari, who ended up sleeping with her *ex*-friend Ron, who wasn't the same Ron that fucked me over except they had the exact same eye brows. But, anyway, that is a whole 'nother story. So anyway, all the girls start runnin' right past the firemen... right into the flaming building to save their mannequin heads... and the firemen were trying to hold all the girls back and like, slapping them, like literally, to kind of bring them back into reality. But it was really weird because we could like see the heads burning one by one and they totally looked real. Anyway, Marcie totally freaked and ran past the firemen and into the building to get Clari, and I started feeling really guilty, because I was just standing there like, letting Suzanne melt to death. So Marcie comes flying out of the place with just one head on her shoulder... Clari. Like... she couldn't even try to save Suzanne while she was in there? Like how much does a mannequin head weigh? Would it have killed her to just pick her up by the hair and bring her out with her? Anyway, so she comes running out of the building carrying Clari and screaming; "She's fire retarded, she's fire retarded!" Excuse me, da. "Retarded?" Like she didn't even know the word "retardant" or anything.

So, Clari ended up being the only head that didn't burn because Marcie's geeky father had some kind of weird, other worldly foresight to spray her with all this *retardant* stuff. Anyway, so the place totally burns down and Marcie's the only one left with a mannequin head.

Well... I wouldn't have done what I did if she didn't deserve it, but Marcie was like gloating for days afterward. So... I kind of stole her mannequin head Clari and brought her down to Lincoln Woods, where we used to play spin the bottle and stuff, and I kind of like... hacked her apart with my father's axe. I wasn't like... enjoying it or anything, but it did feel really good. Marcie drew these geeky eyes on Clari to make her look like her, and she even painted this smug little smile on her face. Well, I just kept hacking away until she was like in hundreds of little pieces, and then I poured some gas on her and lit her up. She wasn't fire "retarded" anymore, I could tell you that much. Nothing is when you pour gas on it.

So anyway, Marcie and me are friends again. I think she just thought her little brother stole her head, but the point is, life goes on and you just have to move on and avsha is gonna have like a huge re-opening next year and until then I'm just kinda, you know, sitting around and stuff. But I'll tell you one thing; when I get my new head, I'm gonna dunk that thing in whatever it takes to keep it from burning and if Marcie thinks I would ever save her burning head if Tony's ever burns down again, she could just forget it.

THE KING (who didn't want to sell aluminum siding) AND I

The Characters

ALAN: Twenties

ANNIE: Twenties

The Setting and Time

The play takes place in a garage in Secaucus, New Jersey.

The time is the present.

(As the lights come up, we see Alan with a paper Burger King crown on his head, sitting in the garage, reading a magazine and eating a candy bar. Next to him is an old broom leaning against the chair. Annie enters, pad and pencil in hand)

ANNIE: Alan?
(Alan jumps out of his seat)
ALAN: Yeah?
ANNIE: Oh, sorry. I didn't mean to scare you but... are you Alan Maywalt?
ALAN: Are you from The Bugalite?
ANNIE: Yes.
ALAN: Oh. (He throws down the magazine, picks up the broom, which he holds in a very dignified way. His voice suddenly deepens and resounds with authority) You may enter!
ANNIE: Uhm... thanks. I got your letter at the office, and I thought I'd come over and talk to you.
ALAN: Fair damsel maiden, as you could imagine, I have many ministers and chancellors and lieges of all kinds under my rule. The king himself, does not write letters.
ANNIE: Uhm... why are you talking like that?
ALAN: You may address me as Sire.
ANNIE: But your mother just said your name is Alan.
ALAN: I know no one by that title here.
ANNIE: Well, okay, "Sire." Somebody wrote The Bugalite a letter saying that somebody named Alan, who lives in this garage, here in Secaucus, thinks he's a king.
ALAN: My bonnie lass, I can assure you there is no one in this castle by the name of... what was it?
ANNIE: Alan Maywalt.
ALAN: Alan. Thou hast been mistook.
ANNIE: Well, whoever wrote the letter said it would be a good human interest story. So I came over to cover it.

ALAN: (Suddenly in natural voice) Great, so you'll write it?

ANNIE: Hey, your voice!

ALAN: (Back to king voice) Is not a king allowed to change his voice at will?

ANNIE: Real kings don't say "is not."

ALAN: Look, thou art a fair maiden and a bonnie lass indeed, but thou art getting on the king's nerves really quick. Now, art thou gonna write the piece or what?

ANNIE: Well, the thing is, I'm not really an official writer. I just kinda help around the office, and once in awhile they'll send me out on something.

ALAN: Young miss damsel, hasten thou to your office and fetcheth me a genuine scribe.

ANNIE: What?

ALAN: (A little less kingly) Go getteth me a real writer!

ANNIE: Why, what's wrong with me?

ALAN: No offense fair mistress, but thou art a coffee fetching gofer!

ANNIE: No, I'm not!

ALAN: (Totally back to actual voice) Look, what's your name?

ANNIE: Annie Woodhall.

ALAN: Look, Annie, no offense or anything, but the least your two bit little local rag sheet with a circulation of twenty seven could do, is send me over one of their *real* reporters.

ANNIE: But I am real. And I'm the only one who even wanted to come over here.

ALAN: What do ya mean?

ANNIE: I mean it was my idea to come here. Nobody else wanted to.

ALAN: You mean a guy shuts himself off in his garage for three weeks and thinks he's a king, and nobody thought it was worth doing a couple paragraphs on?

ANNIE: Well, I did.

ALAN: Yeah, but you're not a real reporter.

ANNIE: Well, I'm trying!

ALAN: Oh, man, this is unbelievable!

ANNIE: But you don't think you're a king.

ALAN: How do you know?

ANNIE: Because you're not acting like one now.

ALAN: Oh, God, just forget it. Tell my mother I'll be in in a
minute.

(Annie starts out, turns back. Points toward the broom)

ANNIE: What's that?

ALAN: What?

ANNIE: That.

ALAN: It's a broom.

ANNIE: I know that, but what is it supposed to be?

ALAN: It's supposed to be one of those king things... you
know, those rods that they carry.

ANNIE: Is that what they call them... rods?

ALAN: I don't know. I don't think so. There's another word.

ANNIE: Scepter.

ALAN: What?

ANNIE: Scepter. I think they call those things a scepter.

ALAN: Oh, okay. Well, thanks. I guess I'll see ya.

(Annie starts out again, turns back)

ANNIE: Ya know if it means anything, I am kind of interested.
I would like to know why you're acting like a king.

ALAN: Look, just forget it. It doesn't matter anymore.

ANNIE: But I'm curious, I really am.

ALAN: It's a long story.

ANNIE: That's okay. I don't have a deadline or anything. We
just hand 'em in whenever.

ALAN: Well, whatever I tell you can't be leaked.

ANNIE: What do ya mean?

ALAN: You know, leaked. Let out. Isn't that a newspaper
term.

ANNIE: Well, I'm not sure. I really just help around the office.

ALAN: Well, whatever I say is "off the record."

ANNIE: Oh, I know that one! That's a newspaper term.

ALAN: Yeah, well. The reason I'm doing this is because I
don't want to sell aluminum siding.

ANNIE: Oh.

ALAN: See my father owns Duraside Siding.

ANNIE: Oh I heard of them. "When you decide to side..."

ALAN: "...side with Duraside." Right. Anyway, I've been outa school for awhile, and everything that I've tried to do that isn't somehow connected with aluminum siding has been a miserable failure.

ANNIE: Oh, I'm sorry.

ALAN: That's okay. I mean I don't have anything against aluminum siding personally. I realize there's a need for it, and that it serves a purpose, but I just don't want to sell it. I hate it. I hate aluminum siding.

ANNIE: Geez, that's too bad.

ALAN: Do you know much about it?

ANNIE: What?

ALAN: Aluminum siding.

ANNIE: No, not really.

ALAN: Well, you'd be surprised. There's really more to it than you probably think. I mean there's all different kinds. There's the original designs, "real to touch" wood-like finishes, anti-dent magnesium plated, fiberglass derivative blends...

ANNIE: Wow. It does sound kind of interesting.

ALAN: Yeah it is but I hate it. I hate aluminum siding and I always have. I don't want to be an aluminum siding salesman. Besides, it really doesn't have much of a future, what with all these simulated brick face companies popping up. People would rather have fake brick then fake wood, and I don't blame 'em. I mean I'd rather have real brick then real wood, but I'd also rather have real fake brick then real fake wood. It just looks better. You can't deny it.

ANNIE: I guess not.

ALAN: I don't want to sound ungrateful. I mean I'm thankful for the opportunity, but it's just dawning on me now that I'm not gonna be anything I ever wanted to be. I mean I know that's a pretty common thing in life, but not to me, because this is the first time I ever lived this part of my life. So I'm

ALAN: (Cont) still new to it. I guess I just want a little more time, ya know? If not to figure out a way to do what I want to do, at least to figure out a way to live with myself not doing it, ya know?

ANNIE: Oh yeah. I know exactly. I really hate my life too. I mean I don't mind it, but it's not nearly what I thought it would be. And I kept lowering my expectations too... just like my parents told me to... but the thing is, I couldn't even achieve my lowest expectation. So now what I am supposed to do?

ALAN: I don't know. I mean I'm no philosopher or anything. I mean I know where I am... and that I'm not really smart, and that I'm living in a garage in Secaucus, New Jersey, and that I probably will for the rest of my life. But it just seems to me that people are finding out they're not what they wanted to be younger than ever now. I mean from what I know, people used to be in their mid 40's or something before it would hit 'em. But now people are finding out much younger. And it's harder that way, because you have to live with yourself feeling that way about yourself for a much longer time.

ANNIE: I'm sure it's not all that bad.

ALAN: Oh, I don't mean I think I'm totally gone. I just feel like a "near do well" ya know? But the thing is, I'm not even that. I'm more like a "near do alright," because I'm just barely doing alright. And to tell you the truth, I'd rather just not do if it's just gonna be "alright."

ANNIE: But "alright's" pretty good nowadays.

ALAN: Oh, I know. But I didn't grow up hoping to be alright. I mean when my second grade teacher asked me what I wanted to be when I grew up, I didn't say; "Well, Miss Bartels, I just want to be alright. I just want to have a long weekend once in awhile, or hit the lottery for say fifty bucks every few months." But really, that's what I should've said. Forget being a policeman or the president or something, I think kids should just hope for cable, or smaller student loan payments, or a decent refund check once in awhile.

ANNIE: But this is the real world now, and those little things become as big as the bigger ones were.

ALAN: I know, I know.

ANNIE: It just sounds to me like you don't want to grow up.

ALAN: You're right, I don't. I really don't. Because the older I get, the more I notice that more seems to happen to you in what seems like less time. And it sucks. Time does fly, but that doesn't mean it's taking you with it. I mean look at the astronauts.

ANNIE: The what?

ALAN: The astronauts. You know, the first astronauts. I saw 'em on some battery commercial and they're old men now. I mean the astronauts are old men now! Doesn't that tell us anything?

ANNIE: I don't know.

ALAN: So I thought of a stunt. Anything I could do to just stall things for a little while. So I asked myself; What do I wanna be... I mean really, no holes barred? A king! Why not!? Then I asked myself what was keeping me from being a king? Well, for one thing, I live in Jersey, and Jersey doesn't have a king. Okay, that's one thing. And I don't have any royal blood. Okay, that's two things. So I have a couple problems. So, I decided to just drop it. You know, just go ahead and proclaim myself king of this little garage in Secaucus, New Jersey. I mean when ya think about it, there's always gotta be a first king. And who's there to tell him he could be king? Nobody. He must tell himself. So I did. Now my parents are having doctors come in to talk to me, and my friends think I totally lost it. But, the bottom line is, I'm not selling aluminum siding. At least not for now. So, I'm keeping it back. My finger is in the dike, and I know it's gonna leak soon, but it's all worth it somehow.

ANNIE: So, why did you send the letter to The Bugalite?

ALAN: Because I thought if I got some publicity it might strengthen my kingdom. You know, buy me some more time before the world comes in.

ANNIE: Oh. Well... I could try to write a story even though I'm not an official reporter. But if it'll help, I'll try.

ALAN: God, thanks.

ANNIE: Sure.

ALAN: Why are you being so nice?

ANNIE: I don't know. I guess because I know what ya mean. I mean about trying to keep the world back and all that.

ALAN: Then you don't think I'm crazy?

ANNIE: Oh, sure I do.

ALAN: Oh.

ANNIE: But in a good way.

ALAN: Oh, well... thanks.

ANNIE: Sure.

ALAN: Oh, and if there's... anything I could do for you. Maybe when all this is over I could give you a deal on some siding or something.

ANNIE: That would be great... your highness.

(Alan smiles as the lights fade to black and the music comes up)

THE END

KIRBY'S LAW

The Characters

A MAN: Twenties or thirties

The Setting and Time

To the audience.

The time is the present.

Me and Kirby used to pack out frozen at A&P. You know, frozen is all that stuff like Mrs. Pauls or Gordon's Fish Sticks and all that. We worked there together while we were in high school, and we became pretty good friends... because we saw a lot of each other... goin' to school and then packing out six or seven hours everyday afterward. On our days off we'd ride around on our mopeds or sneak into movies or somethin' like that. Sometimes we'd even go up to my attic and play air guitar. I guess we had to be pretty tight, because there's not many people I'd be willing to look so stupid in front of like that. I mean playing air guitar and mouthing the words. It kinda makes me want to cringe now, but those are the kinds of things we used to do.

Some days we'd even go to the library. Not to read or anything, but because a lot of the girls would hang out there. We would cut little holes in the newspapers we'd pretend to read, and just look at 'im as long as we wanted to without them seein' us. Kirby and me usually had a great time because we had this game, where we'd try to make each other laugh... you know, crack up real loud so the old librarian with the blue hair would come over and give us what she would call our "First Official Warning." Kirby had a kind of theory; he said that there's no place in the world where you're so prone to giggle or... well, fart, as in a library. It was kind of his little scientific law, and it was true. I know it sounds gross, but I never fart or giggle anywhere as much as I do in libraries. Kirby said it had somethin' to do with the quiet or stillness in the air. I don't know. All I know is, Kirby's law is true.

Well, it was around this time that Kirby and me started goin' our separate ways. And I started pickin' up some of those books... you know, like literature and stuff. Partly because I was really interested in 'em, but partly because I

liked the way I thought I looked reading 'em. I started doin' a
lot of stuff back then that was kinda strange. You know,
using words I really didn't know, or reading by candlelight
when I didn't have to, or even smoking a pipe to try to make
myself look older. I used to read books by guys whose names
I couldn't even pronounce. And I read all those books by
those really sad French guys, who wrote how the world's so
full of nothingness and all that. It kinda made sense back
then, because when you're sixteen, and you live in New
Jersey, you kinda feel that way anyway.

Anyway, after awhile I'd sit there in the library with a
pipe in my mouth, and I'd be wearing my dad's old tweed
jacket, and Kirby would come in and sit across from me and
start tryin' to make me laugh. I started to feel real embar-
rassed by 'im to tell ya the truth, because I thought I was
mature by leaps and bounds back then, and that he was just
being a kid. I'd try to talk to him about all those books and
stuff, but he'd just ride me for tryin' to be somethin' I
wasn't. Like my tryin' to be somethin' a little more than what
I was was a bad thing or somethin'.

Anyway, this one time he was sitting across from me, and
he ripped a fart so loud that everybody in the place turned
around, and the blue haired old lady came over and actually
skipped the First Official Warning and asked him to leave.
Well, when he got up, he looked at me like he expected me to
go with 'im... but I didn't. I just stayed there and kept lookin'
in some stupid French novel like I was really reading it. Then
I saw out of the corner of my eye... her, leading him away.
And that was that.

I quit my job at the A&P not long after that. And I started
workin' at the library part time, and we just kinda started
avoiding each other for the whole next year or so. And then,

when I went away to college... I knew I'd never hear from him again, and I didn't. I thought about maybe going back someday and lookin' him up. But, I don't know. I heard awhile ago that he's workin' for New Jersey Transit, and that he's doing pretty good. I'm gonna be a teacher soon, I guess. But it's funny, because there isn't a time when I go into a library to do research or somethin' when I don't think about Kirby's law. Because it's true. It really is.

JIMMY HAS A TENDENCY

The Characters

JIMMY: Twenties, thirties

CHAD BLANKMAN: TV reporter

FRANKLIN DAYNICKERS: Mechanic

REBECCA KITCHEN: Thirties

The Setting and Time

Jimmy's house.

The time is the present.

(As the lights come up, we see Jimmy standing CR. He is still for ten seconds. Then, suddenly, he runs across the stage at full speed and bashes himself directly into a wall. He rebounds off the wall and crashes to the floor in agony. He gets up slowly, resumes his original position and proceeds to bash himself into the wall a second time. Chad enters with a microphone. He faces the audience as though it were a camera. Jimmy has recovered from his second charge and does it a third time. Jimmy does this repeatedly, behind the others, throughout the play)

CHAD: Testing... testing... one... two... testing. Is this thing on? Testing... one... two... alright, what? So where's the Daynickers guy?
(Franklin enters, lost and bewildered. He has a beer wrapped in a brown paper bag)
FRANKLIN: Uh... Mr. Blankman?
CHAD: What?
FRANKLIN: I'm uh... Franklin Daynickers. You all wanted to interview me on the T.V.?
CHAD: Yeah, yeah, great. Stand here. You know this Jimmy guy, right?
FRANKLIN: Well, I guess you could say...
CHAD: Great, great. Okay, listen, when I say "Chad on the beat," we're on. So just relax and act natural and tell us what you know about him, alright?
FRANKLIN: Well, I uh...
CHAD: Great, great. Okay, three... two... one... Aaaand, "Chad on the beat!" Hello, this is Chad on the beat again, and I'm standing here with Mr. Franklin Daynickers who is a life long personal friend of Mr. Jimmy...
FRANKLIN: ...well, actually I uh...
CHAD: ...Mr. Daynickers, isn't it true that you went to school with Jimmy?

FRANKLIN: Well yeah, we graduated kindergarten together I guess.

CHAD: Did he seem an exceptional child, then? (Franklin doesn't grasp it) Did he seem at all "different?" (Still lost) Did he have a tendency toward self destruction or feel the need to run at accelerated speeds into solid, immobile objects?

FRANKLIN: Well, I don't know about that, but uh... Jimmy was always kind of "off the wall"... if ya know what I mean. (Only Franklin laughs, ridiculously, finally realizing no one else is) Yeah, I remember he used to take flying leaps out the window of our classroom. He never made it though. The school put some kind of protective netting just under the window sills in case he ever made it that far.

(Jimmy is still running directly into the wall, perhaps injured, limping now)

CHAD: I see. Was he verbally demonstrative? (Franklin's confused) Did he... say much?

FRANKLIN: Well, I don't know much about that, but... I remember him being a little "lofty headed" ya might say. He was always ranting on about things like uh... you know, unicorns and fairy godmothers and the such. Real kinda faggy stuff like that. I do remember him saying one thing in particular though...

CHAD: Pray tell. (Franklin's confused) Tell us.

FRANKLIN: Well, he said something like uh... "If I could find a place where physical and all other sorts of boundaries didn't exist, where so called "tangible" reality could be defied or proven conclusively, then perhaps there might be no walls anywhere; be them literal or otherwise."

CHAD: And how old was he when he said that?

FRANKLIN: I don't know... four?

CHAD: Well Mr. Daynickers, thank you very much for stopping by.

FRANKLIN: Yeah, uh... my... you know, pleasure and stuff. Profoundly.

(Franklin smiles for the camera and leaves. Jimmy meanwhile, is still bashing himself into the wall and has now started bleeding from his nose. Rebecca Kitchen enters quickly and stands precisely on mark. She smiles into the camera)

CHAD: Oh, also joining us is Ms. Rebecca Kitchen who...

REBECCA: ...that would be "Mrs." Rebecca Kitchen.

CHAD: Oh, excuse me.

REBECCA: Yes, Sir I shall.

CHAD: Thank you. As I was going to say, you knew Jimmy from his first year of high school. Is that correct?

REBECCA: That is Sir, yes.

CHAD: Well, did...

REBECCA: ...that is indeed, entirely correct.

CHAD: Right. Clear on that. Now, did he exhibit any behavior there other than normal? (She seems a little lost) Did he ever do anything strange?

REBECCA: Well, Jimmy used to be into like these sort of mind games, ya know? He'd always be goofin' on me, askin' me things like; "Hey, Rebecca, do you know any horizontal words for vertical?" I mean... what's a girl supposed to say to that?

CHAD: Yes. Are there any particular incidents that you recall concerning Jimmy and yourself that might give us an idea of what kind of person he really is?

(Jimmy is nearing exhaustion. Bleeding profusely. Keeps charging into the wall)

REBECCA: Well yeah, there was this one time when he borrowed his dad's car and was giving me a ride home. He all the sudden leaned on the gas and started heading for as I recall, a very distinct concrete embankment of some kind. We were going about a hundred and twenty miles per hour and this aforementioned embankment just kept gettin' distincter and distincter. Well, I finally convinced him to turn off at the last second, but it was close... very close.

CHAD: Did he ever tell you why he did things like that?

REBECCA: Well, now ya know Chad, upon reflection, I just never really thought to ask. Jimmy's always been a little different from everybody else. He's just never seen things like other people. He just always thought he was different, like he could go through walls or somethin'.

CHAD: (Real fast) Can he?

REBECCA: I don't know where you're gettin' "Kenny" from. My name's Rebecca.

CHAD: No... "can he" go through walls?

REBECCA: No, he can not. I've seen him try once or twice. He's just like everybody else. After awhile he starts bleeding, loses a lot of blood and usually breaks a few bones.

CHAD: So, why does he do it?

REBECCA: Well Chad, you just gotta understand Jimmy. It doesn't matter why he does it. It just matters that he does it. Okay, so there's a man in the very near twenty first century who believes he could go through walls. He tries again and again and it's probably gonna kill him someday. So what? What's the diff Chad? Are there any laws against trying to walk through walls... yet?

CHAD: Well, not that I know of. Well, Mrs. Kitchen, thank you very much for talking with us.

REBECCA: No problemo Chaddo.

(She pinches his butt as she walks off. Chad faces the camera again)

CHAD: Well... this is Chad "on the beat" Blankman, signing off.

(Chad freezes facing the camera with an exaggerated smile. Lights start to fade as we watch Jimmy try one more time to go through the wall. Doesn't make it. Lights go to black as the music comes up)

THE END

LITTLE THINGS

The Characters

A MAN OR WOMAN: Any age

The Setting and Time

To the audience.

The time is the present.

The worst time, or one of the worst, was when she came out after one of her radiation treatments. She was really small, and they were hard on her, but she was holding up pretty good because she basically just had a lot of balls.

Anyway, every once in awhile they would have to mark the area near her neck where they were gonna concentrate the radiation on. They would mark it with this dye... which was sort of like the color of dried blood.

Well, this one time, one of the last times they bothered, they messed up. They splattered some of the dye on her chin when they were marking her. It wasn't much, just a few tiny drops, but you could see 'em pretty good. Well, when she came out of the room, the first thing I saw was those little spots. And she saw that I saw 'em, and it made her kind of nervous. So, we went into the bathroom there and put some of that powdered soap on one of those hard paper towels. Well, she tried for awhile to rub those marks out, but she couldn't. I kept telling her that they were coming off, but they weren't. Then she started getting kind of panicky. I mean she was hurting herself, trying to rub this stuff off her face... and I had to stop her. It wouldn't come off, no matter how hard we tried.

There aren't many things I guess, that you know you'll remember forever, but I don't think I'll ever forget how she looked at herself when she saw those spots on her face. See I guess everybody has a kind of limit of what they can take, and then you just can't take it anymore. And I knew after that, I thought anyway, that something changed in her. I felt like after that, she gave up in some way. I mean sometimes little things like that on top of bigger ones can be the things that end up killing you.

21st CENTURY FOX

The Characters

DIRECTOR: B Movie maker

ACTRESS: Young woman

CAMERAMAN: A man with a real or imaginary camera

PROPMAN: A man any age

The Setting and Time

A movie set. Facing the audience is a hanging window suspended by three lengths of fishing wire. There is a table set with dishes.

The time is the present.

(As the lights come up, the director enters and stands in front of the audience, smoking. The others wander on the set and ready themselves for the shoot. The director turns to the actress...)

DIRECTOR: You realize this is it, don't ya babe? This is the day. The shot. The moment. The summit, peak, climax of this venture. This is not the day before, not the day after, this is the day, the hour, the minute, the second. Do you grasp what it is I'm trying to convey to you?

ACTRESS: Uhm...

DIRECTOR: This is no picnic, this is nuclear destruction. Grasp?

ACTRESS: Well...

DIRECTOR: We're not sugar coating anything here. I need it all from you. I need to see it on your face. The fear, dread, horror, terror, dismay, just general discomfort, okay?

ACTRESS: Absolu...

DIRECTOR: Great, let's do it! This is the first time you realize "it" has happened. You feel the room shake. You feel a kind of warmness. You glance at your various household items; your fine china, it's being destroyed! It's a lot like an earth-quake, I know, believe me, I have done lots of research. (To cameraman) Okay, you pan in on the dish. (To propman) You shake the table and keep yourself out of the shot. Alright! Lights! (Lights up) Aaaaaaaand... nuke it! (Clap OS, the director turns to cameraman) Okay, start shaking. (He shakes camera) Okay, come in on her face. (To actress) C'mon, baby, let's see the fear, let's see the utter terror. (She tries, but not convincingly) Babe, feel the anger, look at your expensive china! What if it breaks!? (To cameraman) Pan in on the china, slowly. (He shoots china, propman under the table shaking it) Shake it! Shake it!... No! Cut! Slice! Castrate! Cut! Cut! Cut! (Pause, to actress) There's nothing. I don't feel it. I mean, what's the matter?

ACTRESS: I'm sorry. I just can't connect. I don't know what
to draw on. I mean I've never experienced this kind of thing.

DIRECTOR: Look, I told you. This is it. This is what it's like.
We need to catch it on your face. Let's try a little exercise.
C'mere. (She moves over to him, they both face audience)
Okay, give me happy. (She gives appropriate facial expression) Sad, (She gives sad), Jealous, (She gives jealous),
thoughtful, (She gives thoughtful), in love, (She gives in
love), okay, now give me nuclear destruction, (She gives the
same expression as sad), That's it! That's it, baby! Now hold
that. You got it. Ready to try again?

ACTRESS: (Frozen in expression) I guess.

DIRECTOR: Alright. (To propman) Try shaking the table a
little harder. Don't be afraid to break anything. It's about
time Hollywood got a kick in the ass. I don't mind making a
downer film. We'll scare the shit out of them at Cannes. (To
actress) I need the expression, then I need the pan on the
china. We have to get this. This is horror. This is hell. Are
we ready? Aaaaaand... lights! (Lights up) Do it! (Cameraman
starts shooting her, shaking camera) That's good, that's good.
Get her face. That's it. That's it. (To actress) C'mon, babe...
horror! That is fine china! That is Bloomingdales, non-refun-
dable! (To cameraman) Okay, come in slowly on china. Yes,
yes, closer... closer... (To propman) Shake it! Shake it!
(Propman shaking the table from under) C'mon, c'mon!
(Finally a piece of china falls off and breaks) Alright, pan on
broken china! Pan on broken china! Now freeze, hold it there
aaaaaaaaand out! Nice work, people. Thank you ladies and
gentlemen. One more shot and we'll wrap it up for the day.
It's the window scene. Yes, the all important window scene.
The very cornerstone of this project. (To actress) You glance
at the window. Your world is falling apart. (To propman)
You do the thing with the window and stay the hell out of the
shot. (To cameraman) You pan in. (To actress) Do you know
what happens here? You hear this big kind of wind, a nuclear

DIRECTOR: (Cont) radium gaseous wind! You glance at the window. Suddenly it explodes, shattering! Scream, fall to your knees, duck and cover. (The propman slides under the window, out of view of the camera. He is lying on the ground ready to break the window with his little hammer) Alright, let's shoot it! Ready!? Lights... (Lights up) Aaaaaaaaand... do it! (To cameraman) That's it. Shake it now, baby!

ACTRESS: Oh my God! Oh my God!

DIRECTOR: That's it, feel the horror! You hear the wind coming. (Director blows in the direction of the actress) Look at the window. Here comes the wind! Here comes the wind! Aaaaaand... (The propman tries to break the window timidly with his tiny hammer, but it won't break) What is that! Where's the shattering! Where's the wind!? Cut it! (To propman) What the hell is going on here? I need the pivotal nucleon wind radium effect!

PROPMAN: Sorry.

(The director goes into the corner. Pouts. Silence)

DIRECTOR: Alright. One more time. This is it. They are gonna love this. Alright, places. Quiet! Lights please! (Lights up) Aaaaaaaand... commence! (Camera on actress) That's it. You're horrified, baby. Yeah, yeah, that is beautiful. You glance toward the window... in a sense, "the window of life"... (To cameraman) Pan in slowly on window. (Cameraman remains still, dozing off) The window! Pan to the window! (He pans to window) Yes! Yes! Now, here it comes! Here comes the wind! Aaaaaaaaand...

(Pause, then the propman again timidly taps the window, trying to break it. The director collapses in exasperation as we continue to hear the little hammer taps against the glass as the lights fade slowly to black and the music comes up)

THE END

About the Author

Charles Evered's first full length work, THE SIZE OF THE WORLD, won him The Berrilla Kerr Award. He is also the recipient of The Eugene O'Neill, Audrey Wood, and George Pierce Baker scholarships, the first writer at Yale to be awarded all three. Also while at Yale, he was named the recipient of The Hendon and Lortel scholarships. His one act play, "Running Funny," won him The Crawford Award. Mr. Evered is also the recipient of The Chesterfield, Albee and Millay Colony writing fellowships. He is the "Writer in Residence" at The New Jersey Shakespeare Festival and has written screenplays for Steven Spielberg's Dreamworks, Arthur Hiller's Golden Quill, Disney and Universal Pictures, among others. As a director, he has staged several original plays and was awarded the "Best of the New Generation" Award at The Williamstown Theatre Festival. He is a graduate of Rutgers University, where he studied anthropology, as well as Yale University, where he was awarded a master's degree. He serves in the United States Air Force Reserves.